OPP
VIE
SER

Illeg

Other Books of Related Interest:

Opposing Viewpoints Series

Canada

Interracial America

Mexico

Population

Current Controversies Series

Drug Trafficking

Illegal Immigration

The Uninsured

At Issue Series

Health Care Legislation

How Can the Poor Be Helped?

Should the United States Be Multilingual?

"Congress shall make no law . . . abridging the freedom of speech, or of the press."

First Amendment to the US Constitution

The basic foundation of our democracy is the First Amendment guarantee of freedom of expression. The Opposing Viewpoints Series is dedicated to the concept of this basic freedom and the idea that it is more important to practice it than to enshrine it.

OPPOSING VIEWPOINTS® SERIES

Illegal Immigration

David Haugen and Susan Musser, Book Editors

GREENHAVEN PRESS
A part of Gale, Cengage Learning

GALE
CENGAGE Learning™

Detroit • New York • San Francisco • New Haven, Conn • Waterville, Maine • London

Christine Nasso, *Publisher*
Elizabeth Des Chenes, *Managing Editor*

© 2011 Greenhaven Press, a part of Gale, Cengage Learning.

Gale and Greenhaven Press are registered trademarks used herein under license.

For more information, contact:
Greenhaven Press
27500 Drake Rd.
Farmington Hills, MI 48331-3535
Or you can visit our Internet site at gale.cengage.com

For product information and technology assistance, contact us at

Gale Customer Support, 1-800-877-4253
For permission to use material from this text or product, submit all requests online at
www.cengage.com/permissions

Further permissions questions can be emailed to permissionrequest@cengage.com

Articles in Greenhaven Press anthologies are often edited for length to meet page requirements. In addition, original titles of these works are changed to clearly present the main thesis and to explicitly indicate the author's opinion. Every effort is made to ensure that Greenhaven Press accurately reflects the original intent of the authors. Every effort has been made to trace the owners of copyrighted material.

Cover image copyright © William Albert Allard/National Geographic/Getty Images.

LIBRARY OF CONGRESS CATALOGING-IN-PUBLICATION DATA

Illegal immigration / David Haugen and Susan Musser, book editors.
    p. cm. -- (Opposing viewpoints)
    Includes bibliographical references and index.
    ISBN 978-0-7377-5225-0 (hardcover) -- ISBN 978-0-7377-5226-7 (pbk.)
    1. United States--Emigration and immigration. 2. Immigrants--United States. 3. Illegal aliens--United States. I. Haugen, David M., 1969- II. Musser, Susan.
    JV6465.I446 2011
    325.73--dc22
                                                                    2010054415

Printed in the United States of America
1 2 3 4 5 6 7 15 14 13 12 11

Contents

Chapter 3: Should US Immigration Policy Be Reformed?

Chapter 4: Are Illegal Immigrants Treated Fairly in the United States?

Why Consider Opposing Viewpoints?

> "The only way in which a human being can make some approach to knowing the whole of a subject is by hearing what can be said about it by persons of every variety of opinion and studying all modes in which it can be looked at by every character of mind. No wise man ever acquired his wisdom in any mode but this."
>
> John Stuart Mill

In our media-intensive culture it is not difficult to find differing opinions. Thousands of newspapers and magazines and dozens of radio and television talk shows resound with differing points of view. The difficulty lies in deciding which opinion to agree with and which "experts" seem the most credible. The more inundated we become with differing opinions and claims, the more essential it is to hone critical reading and thinking skills to evaluate these ideas. Opposing Viewpoints books address this problem directly by presenting stimulating debates that can be used to enhance and teach these skills. The varied opinions contained in each book examine many different aspects of a single issue. While examining these conveniently edited opposing views, readers can develop critical thinking skills such as the ability to compare and contrast authors' credibility, facts, argumentation styles, use of persuasive techniques, and other stylistic tools. In short, the Opposing Viewpoints Series is an ideal way to attain the higher-level thinking and reading skills so essential in a culture of diverse and contradictory opinions.

In addition to providing a tool for critical thinking, Opposing Viewpoints books challenge readers to question their own strongly held opinions and assumptions. Most people form their opinions on the basis of upbringing, peer pressure, and personal, cultural, or professional bias. By reading carefully balanced opposing views, readers must directly confront new ideas as well as the opinions of those with whom they disagree. This is not to simplistically argue that everyone who reads opposing views will—or should—change his or her opinion. Instead, the series enhances readers' understanding of their own views by encouraging confrontation with opposing ideas. Careful examination of others' views can lead to the readers' understanding of the logical inconsistencies in their own opinions, perspective on why they hold an opinion, and the consideration of the possibility that their opinion requires further evaluation.

Evaluating Other Opinions

To ensure that this type of examination occurs, Opposing Viewpoints books present all types of opinions. Prominent spokespeople on different sides of each issue as well as well-known professionals from many disciplines challenge the reader. An additional goal of the series is to provide a forum for other, less known, or even unpopular viewpoints. The opinion of an ordinary person who has had to make the decision to cut off life support from a terminally ill relative, for example, may be just as valuable and provide just as much insight as a medical ethicist's professional opinion. The editors have two additional purposes in including these less known views. One, the editors encourage readers to respect others' opinions—even when not enhanced by professional credibility. It is only by reading or listening to and objectively evaluating others' ideas that one can determine whether they are worthy of consideration. Two, the inclusion of such viewpoints encourages the important critical thinking skill of objectively evaluating an author's credentials and bias. This evaluation will illuminate an author's reasons for taking a particular stance on an issue and will aid in readers' evaluation of the author's ideas.

It is our hope that these books will give readers a deeper understanding of the issues debated and an appreciation of the complexity of even seemingly simple issues when good and honest people disagree. This awareness is particularly important in a democratic society such as ours in which people enter into public debate to determine the common good. Those with whom one disagrees should not be regarded as enemies but rather as people whose views deserve careful examination and may shed light on one's own.

Thomas Jefferson once said that "difference of opinion leads to inquiry, and inquiry to truth." Jefferson, a broadly educated man, argued that "if a nation expects to be ignorant and free . . . it expects what never was and never will be." As individuals and as a nation, it is imperative that we consider the opinions of others and examine them with skill and discernment. The Opposing Viewpoints Series is intended to help readers achieve this goal.

David L. Bender and Bruno Leone,
Founders

Introduction

> *"I believe we can put politics aside and finally have an immigration system that's accountable. I believe we can appeal not to people's fears but to their hopes, to their highest ideals, because that's who we are as Americans."*
>
> —Barack Obama,
> Remarks by the President on
> Comprehensive Immigration Reform,
> July 1, 2010.

> *"A sizable number of Americans oppose reform, see it as dangerous to the economy and their well-being, and would be just as happy to send illegal immigrants home and board up the border."*
>
> —Luisita Lopez Torregrosa,
> Politics Daily website, July 1, 2010.

In a July 1, 2010, speech on immigration reform presented at the American University School of International Service in Washington, D.C., US president Barack Obama disparaged America's immigration policies and the flaws in a system that keeps legal immigration applicants waiting for years while numerous illegal aliens sneak across the nation's borders each day. "The system is broken. And everybody knows it," Obama stated in his address. Blaming congressional inaction and the "wrangling" of special interest groups for thwarting any meaningful policy change, Obama noted that border states are taking matters into their own hands and passing laws that might violate human rights in the pursuit of stemming the tide of illegal immigrants. Decrying such a patchwork response to immigration problems, the president declared that it is Washington that must lead by example: "Our task ... is to make our national laws actually work—to shape a system that reflects our values as a nation of laws and a nation of immigrants."

In his speech, Obama detailed his vision of how the laws of the United States must operate to fix the broken system. He advocates a "path toward citizenship" for those noncriminal aliens living and working in the country. He maintains this path must entail that illegal immigrants admit they broke the law and pay a fine to atone for their transgression. He favors the passage of the Development, Relief and Education for Alien Minors (DREAM) Act, a proposed piece of legislation that would grant citizenship to alien children who enroll in and acquire a degree from an institute of higher education or who serve honorably for two years in the military. Finally, the president supports stiffer enforcement measures at the nation's borders, including the hiring of more border patrol agents and other personnel to perform tracking and intelligence work especially in the Southwest. Despite Obama's desire to create bipartisan agreement among legislators, members of Congress are still locked in debate over the issue of how to treat illegal immigrants already in America, and a "path toward citizenship" bill has routinely failed to pass.

Many Republican members of Congress have rejected the president's call for what they see as a "blanket amnesty" for illegal immigrants living within the United States. A month before Obama gave his speech at the School of International Service, eight Republican senators wrote a letter to the president, urging him not to go through with an alternative amnesty plan—one that would avoid legislators' approval—if the congressional bill continued to fail. Fox News reported on June 23, 2010, that part of the letter warned, "Such a move would further erode the American public's confidence in the federal government and its commitment to securing the borders and enforcing the laws already on the books." Exactly how amnesty would threaten the nation is taken up by groups like the Federation for American Immigration Reform (FAIR). According to the FAIR website, amnesty would burden America with millions of new poor people, cost taxpayers millions of dollars in welfare services, jeopardize national security, and make a mockery of the legal paths to immigration. Perhaps most gallingly, in its opinion, "an amnesty says that eventually you will be forgiven, even rewarded, for breaking the law."

While President Obama believes amnesty should be part of any comprehensive immigration reform bill, his administration still stresses the tightening of borders and crackdowns on US employers who take advantage of the numerous illegal immigrants who must work to survive. In early August 2010, Senate Democrats pushed a bill through Congress that earmarked $600 million to beef up border security by hiring fifteen hundred more border patrol agents. Spearheaded by Senator Chuck Schumer, a Democrat from New York and a proponent of comprehensive immigration reform, the bill hoped to prove Democrats' commitment to reform measures beyond amnesty. Speaking before the Senate on August 12, Schumer stated, "In addition to providing many vital resources for securing our southern border . . . this bill is also enormously important because it will clear the path for restarting the bipartisan discussions we absolutely need to have on how best to restore the rule of law to our entire immigration system." Conservatives are not convinced, though, that the $600 million bill will build a bridge between parties on the issue of immigration reform. "If that's what [Democrat leaders] had in mind, they're going to be disappointed," Mark Krikorian, executive director of the pro-enforcement Center for Immigration Studies, told the *Washington Independent* on August 6, 2010. "The border hasn't been secured, they just passed a piece of legislation. Until border control measures have been not only legislated but fully litigated, you can't even start a discussion on legalization."

Meanwhile, federal border security bills are not popular among immigrant groups within the United States, and Democratic politicians tend to lose support from Latinos when they back strong anti-immigrant legislation. Hispanic organizations have also taken up the fight against state laws—such as the 2010 Arizona law SB 1070, which allows police officers to demand proof of citizenship from any person lawfully stopped, detained, or arrested—that have filled the void left by congressional inaction. In a July 12, 2010, press release, the National Council of La Raza, the largest national Hispanic civil rights organization in the United States, argued, "Like no other issue, immigration has been manipulated to demonize Latinos and challenge their place in America, regardless of their immigration status. And SB 1070, which legalizes and legitimizes racial profiling, has become the prime vehicle for that strategy—a false solution to a real problem." Most Hispanic organizations do not advocate illegal immigration, but they do point out that most border crossers are not bad people; Mexican and Central American immigrants come to the United States because it offers the hope of economic opportunity and, perhaps, a chance to reunite with family members that have already established themselves in the country. These organizations worry that laws that give police the power to inspect a person's immigration status will simply draw a discriminatory dividing line between Latinos and the rest of America.

In *Opposing Viewpoints: Illegal Immigration*, Matthew Rothschild, editor of the *Progressive*, a liberal news magazine, argues that Arizona's SB 1070 exposes the prejudice inherent in American politics and society. Placed in a chapter titled How Should America Enforce Its Borders? Rothschild's opinion piece stirs the debate surrounding the motivation for stricter border security. In other chapters titled How Does Illegal Immigration Impact America? Should US Immigration Policy Be Reformed? and Are Illegal Immigrants Treated Fairly in the United States? various other voices debate the broad spectrum of issues relating to illegal immigration and impending immigration reform. The contending views and the diversity of the subject matter suggest that immigration reform will not happen overnight. President Obama's call for a reform policy that "reflects our values as a nation of laws and a nation of immigrants" seems to beg for bipartisan agreement on what those values are, and so far, the various political and ethnic groups involved in this issue expound differing concerns and agendas when it comes to defining the status, contributions, and burdens of illegal immigrants in America.

OPPOSING
VIEWPOINTS®
SERIES

CHAPTER 1

How Does Illegal Immigration Impact America?

Chapter Preface

In 1892 the United States opened Ellis Island, an immigration station in New York Harbor that has come to symbolize the multiethnic composition of the country and the blending of many heritages into one American identity. Though closed in 1954, Ellis Island still represents "the golden door" that Emma Lazarus referred to in her famous poem inscribed at the base of the Statue of Liberty. The island witnessed the orderly processing of foreigners—predominantly European— who sought legal immigration into a country that promised new hope and freedom to the world's poor and downtrodden; however, the influx of immigrants that flooded the station in the early 1900s dried to a trickle by the 1920s when Congress began passing immigration quotas that cut the number of arriving immigrants from around 1 million per year down to less than 160,000 per year.

At the same time that quota laws were restricting European and Asian immigration levels, several hundred thousand Mexicans fled the revolution in their country and sought a new life across their northern border. Though US ranchers in California, New Mexico, Arizona, and Texas employed these immigrants in droves, several local and state watchdogs warned that the influx was breeding crime in border communities and straining public services funded by taxes (which the immigrants were not paying). The vice president of the California Federation of Labor, Edward H. Dowell, told Congress in 1928 that illegal immigration from Mexico was unfairly burdening his state and other border states. A year later, the United States entered the Great Depression, and lawmakers clamped down on work visas to stem Mexican immigration. The measure may have been unnecessary because with so little work available, many Mexican laborers voluntarily returned to their homeland.

In the mid-twentieth century, when prosperity returned to the United States, Mexican immigration also resumed. Illegal immigrants poured across the border to grab agricultural jobs during the worker shortages precipitated by World War II. Ranchers and farmers along the border prospered from the influx of cheap labor and did everything in their power to keep illegal aliens from being deported. One Texas border patrol agent working in the 1950s told the *Christian Science Monitor* in a July 6, 2006, article, "When we caught illegal aliens on farms and ranches, the farmer or rancher would often call and complain [to officials in El Paso]. And depending on how politically connected they were, there would be political intervention."

Since the 1950s, America has continued to struggle with immigration problems across its southern border. As the viewpoints in the following chapter attest, concerns about immigrants burdening public welfare and stealing American jobs is matched by a desire for a growing workforce and a belief in America as a beacon for the world's huddled masses. For some Americans, the threat is that the golden door has been flung wide open, and the orderly process of acquiring citizenship has been replaced by contempt for the law. As legal immigrant Boris Epshteyn told FoxNews.com on May 5, 2010, "Illegal aliens disrespect the American rule of law. They disrespect legal immigrants like me who stood in line to come here. And they disrespect all American citizens at large who are kept safe by the immigration rules and processes." Others, however, believe the "threat" of illegal immigrants is based on unsound fears. Nick Gillespie, the managing editor of *Reason* magazine, told readers in its August/September 2006 issue that "a vanishingly small proportion of illegal immigrants come here to live in the shadows of American prosperity." According to Gillespie, 98 percent of illegal-alien respondents to a 2005 National Immigration Forum survey in Miami, Los Angeles, and Chicago said they would legalize their status if given the opportunity. Such an amnesty has been proposed many times, but the idea still rankles with those who believe that excusing illegal immigration is not the path to eliminating the supposed dangers it imposes on American society and the nation's legal policies.

❘ *"Job displacement is the handmaid of illegal immigration."*

Illegal Immigration Threatens the American Economy

Michael E. Telzrow

As the United States slipped into a recession in 2007, the impact of illegal immigration on the economy came to the forefront of debates concerning the looming financial crisis. While some argued that illegal immigrants help drive and aid the American economy, many remained resolute that immigrants' presence in the country only weakens the already struggling economy further. In the viewpoint that follows, Michael E. Telzrow takes the latter position and argues that the costs of illegal immigration far outweigh any benefits it provides for the American economy. Telzrow contends that illegal immigration especially harms American workers by driving down wages and displacing them from their jobs. In addition, the author asserts that illegal immigrants' acceptance of such low wages has led to their depen-

Michael E. Telzrow, "The True Cost of 'Cheap' Labor: The Costs Associated with Uncontrolled Immigration and the Flooding of the U.S. Job Market with Foreign, Low-Wage Laborers Far Outweigh Any Savings to Be Gained," *New American*, February 19, 2007. Reprinted by permission.

dence on federal aid programs, further burdening the economy. Michael E. Telzrow has a master's degree in history and museum studies and has written numerous articles on history, culture, and politics.

As you read, consider the following questions:

1. What example does Telzrow present to support his claim that American workers will do the same jobs as illegal immigrants if they are paid fairly?

2. According to the figures of Philip L. Martin, cited by the author, by how many dollars would food costs increase for the average American household if the number of illegal immigrants in the fields was decreased?

3. What is the estimated net cost of post-1969 immigration, and how much of this total cost is attributed to illegal immigration, as stated by Telzrow?

One of the great myths of the immigration debate is that American workers will not do the types of jobs currently being filled in large part by illegal immigrants. A corollary to this train of thought is that the historically unprecedented levels of immigration, much of it illegal, benefits the U.S. economy and improves our standard of living.

Proponents of this school of thought rarely put forth facts or figures to support their assertion, instead they simply point to the preponderance of recent immigrants in unskilled and low-paying jobs as de facto proof that Americans refuse to do what is traditionally considered menial labor. As a result, some in the business community, supported by the U.S. Chamber of Commerce, clamor for a liberal guest-worker program[1] based upon the assumption that without one, America will face a long-term labor shortage and economic ruin. This enormous

1. Guest-worker programs are designed to allow non-US citizens to work in the United States, typically on a temporary basis.

megaphone of unchallenged opinion has partially succeeded in convincing Americans that without continued access to millions of foreign workers, America's economy will wither on the vine, and that the best way to stop illegal immigration is to pass guest-worker legislation.

Illegal Immigration Drives Down Wages

One of the most fraudulent economic claims regarding immigration comes from the agricultural industry. For years we have been led to believe that the market for seasonal agricultural workers remains very tight, despite the massive influx of alien workers, and that any reduction of labor would result in skyrocketing consumer costs. But in 1993, the bipartisan Commission on Agricultural Workers determined that an oversupply of workers existed. Since then, successive governmental and nonpartisan commissions have come to the same conclusion—the seasonal agricultural market is literally awash with willing workers. There is no shortage, and even if there were a tight market, this would improve wages and benefits and do more to lift workers out of poverty than any of the social-welfare schemes foisted upon Americans since the 1960s.

On the surface, the claim that native-born Americans will not perform seasonal agricultural work and other "hard labor" jobs appears true. But it is not because Americans fear hard work. The fact is that poor Americans are not willing to work for depressed wages when state-sponsored welfare is readily available. Increasing numbers of illegal aliens drive down wages and make working in the fields or packing plants less attractive to American workers.

A recent illegal immigration crackdown at a number of Swift & Company meat-packing plants across the country illustrates the economic point that Americans will, when paid more than a sub-subsistence wage, fill the so-called undesirable jobs that only recent immigrants will take. Almost immediately after hundreds of illegal workers were rounded up, creating an actual tight market, Swift & Company officials increased wages by $1.95 per hour to attract legal workers. The results were predictable. U.S. citizens queued up by the hundreds outside the doors of Swift & Company employment offices for the chance to do the difficult work that experts tell us American citizens will no longer do.

Job displacement is the handmaid of illegal immigration. According to a 1993 report of the Commission on Agricultural Workers, native peach-industry workers in Georgia, many of them African American, were displaced by Hispanic migrants. Additional reports by the commission noted that migrants replaced natives and previous immigrants in the cucumber and apple industries in Michigan. The commission documented another case in which mechanized agricultural packing houses in Michigan ceased operations after switching to manual packing in the field. The unionized native workers were eliminated almost overnight, their jobs replaced by lower-paid field hands from south of the border. The glut of illegal aliens suppressed wages, shut out American workers, and consigned newly arrived immigrants to a life of impoverishment. The same holds true on a larger scale today [in 2007].

Consumer Savings Are Minimal

Proponents of guest-worker legislation maintain that it is just and right to use labor from Mexico. They claim that U.S. consumers benefit from low-wage farm labor in the form of low supermarket prices. But the consumer price benefits are small because the labor cost is only part of the total cost. In any case, the price benefits at the supermarket are outweighed by costs associated with healthcare, law enforcement, and education.

In 1996, agricultural economists at Iowa State estimated that the removal of illegal workers from the work force would prompt a short-term 6 percent price increase at the supermarket for summer and fall produce, gradually decreasing to a 3 percent intermediate-term increase. And even this figure may be overstated. Relying on a native labor force and legal temporary workers during the winter-spring season would reduce the increases by half.

According to Philip L. Martin, Ph.D., professor of Agriculture and Resource Economics at UC [University of California]-Davis, the average household in 2004 spent about $370 per year on fresh produce. In an article entitled "How We Eat: 2004," Martin posits that a tightening of the agricultural labor market, achieved by decreasing the number of aliens in the field, would lead to a 40 percent increase in farm labor wages, and a mere $9 per year increase in food costs to the average American household. On the other hand, farm laborers would enjoy an increase in earnings that would lift them above the poverty line, and make the use of welfare less attractive.

A tight labor market in which employees are at a premium is preferable to a surplus labor market. Worker wages and benefits improve, not as a result of government interference but in the natural economic context in which workers are paid in harmony with their true value.

Illegals Drain Welfare Programs

Amnesty proponents also make great use of the moral high ground, claiming that the United States has an ethical duty to lift illegal migrants out of poverty. But what is the moral justification for displacing native workers and consigning recent immigrants, legal or otherwise, to a life of poverty in low-wage, dead-end jobs, so that agribusinesses may increase their profits while the average American saves mere pennies at the supermarket? Most Americans would welcome an insignificant increase at the supermarket, and a higher quality of life for farm laborers, if it meant reducing the costs associated with runaway illegal immigration.

The costs associated with uncontrolled immigration far outweigh any savings gained from the use of low-wage labor.

Illegal Immigrant Population by State

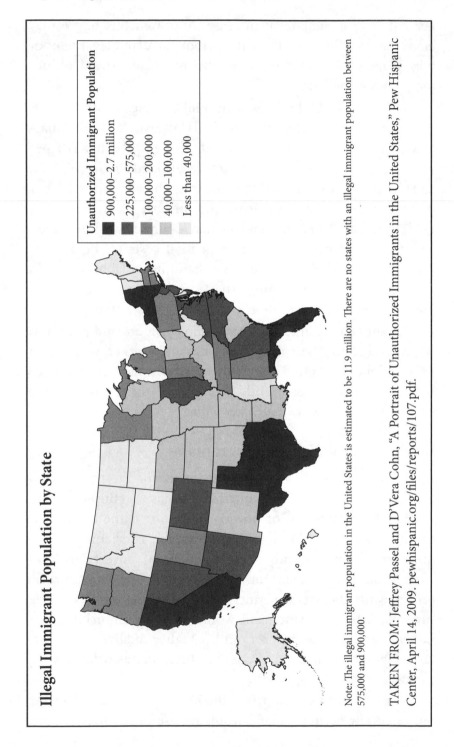

Unauthorized Immigrant Population

- 900,000–2.7 million
- 225,000–575,000
- 100,000–200,000
- 40,000–100,000
- Less than 40,000

Note: The illegal immigrant population in the United States is estimated to be 11.9 million. There are no states with an illegal immigrant population between 575,000 and 900,000.

TAKEN FROM: Jeffrey Passel and D'Vera Cohn, "A Portrait of Unauthorized Immigrants in the United States," Pew Hispanic Center, April 14, 2009. pewhispanic.org/files/reports/107.pdf.

According to a March 2005 Current Population Survey by the U.S. Census Bureau, statistics indicate that 29 percent of immigrant-headed households use at least one major welfare program, compared with 18 percent for native households. Equally disturbing is the low level of education and high level of poverty that characterize recent immigrants. The poverty rate for immigrants and their U.S.-born children stands at 18.4 percent—fully 57 percent higher than that of the native population. It is true that, as in the past immigration patterns, immigrants make economic progress the longer that they live in the United States, but even after 15 years they still suffer from higher rates of poverty, and utilize welfare programs more than natives.

Recent estimates indicate that the net cost (after tax contributions are subtracted) of post-1969 immigration approached $61 billion in 2000, of which $35 billion was attributed to illegal immigration. In 1996, a study by the National Bureau of Economic Research revealed that the total annual immigrant welfare benefits receipts totaled $180 billion! These numbers are sure to increase as the current wave of immigration shows no sign of abating.

True Cost Must Be Measured

The true cost of runaway immigration cannot be measured solely in economic terms. There is a social dimension that threatens to undermine the fabric of our nation. The educational level of recent immigrants is far below that of the native population. In 2005, fully 31 percent of recent adult immigrants lacked a high-school diploma—a figure more than three times that of the native population. Over a third of immigrants lack health insurance, accounting for three-fourths of the uninsured population since 1989.

So what is the true social and economic impact of uncontrolled immigration, whether it is legal or illegal? We must ask ourselves if it is truly in the nation's best interest to allow millions of foreign workers to flood certain segments of the job market under the misconception that such activity is needed to sustain the U.S. economy. And where is the wisdom in driving down wages, forcing native workers out, and creating a permanent foreign-born underclass? Division and social unrest cannot be far behind such a model. Finally, can a nation that has largely abandoned its formerly successful assimilation model expect to sustain itself as a united entity? These questions, and others, are largely absent from the current debate, and we ignore them at our own peril.

"*Excluding the positive economic impact of lower undocumented migrant wages from the equation is like declaring the 8.1 billion hours of free service by America's 61 million volunteers as economically irrelevant.*"

Illegal Immigration Strengthens the American Economy

John Price

In the following viewpoint, John Price, the president and cofounder of the business intelligence firm InfoAmericas located in Latin America, makes the case that illegal immigrants in America contribute significantly to the national economy and provide many benefits to both employers and American consumers. Price critiques the view that undocumented workers add to the American deficit in lost tax revenue and disproportionate use of federal welfare programs, claiming that in fact they provide increased tax revenue from businesses whose taxable profits are a direct result of the decreased wages paid to undocumented employees. These decreased wages further result in aggregate savings for the

John Price, "Development Economics Upside-Down: How Latin America Subsidizes the American Way of Life," Perspectives on the Americas, Center for Hemispheric Policy at the University of Miami, November 9, 2007. Reprinted by permission.

average household, according to Price, which can be seen in the discounted prices of products and services. Price also states that many illegal workers opt out of welfare programs even though they contribute earnings to them, thus adding to the coffers for the American workers who collect from programs such as Medicaid, veteran benefits, and Social Security.

As you read, consider the following questions:

1. As stated by Price, what are "the strongest fiscal and financial arguments" ignored by critics of illegal immigration?

2. According to the author, how much do illegal immigrants save home builders per household?

3. How much does Price estimate the collective work effort of illegal immigrants generates in savings for both American businesses and consumers?

The growing populist sentiment in the United States against illegal immigration likes to point out that not only do these migrants steal U.S. jobs, they also send $50 billion back to Latin America each year instead of spending it in the United States. In fact, the approximately $2,000 per year sent home by the average working illegal migrant is less than 15% of what he earns in the United States and far less than what he contributes to the U.S. economy. A lesser known fact is that wealthy Latin Americans hold $1.9 trillion in U.S. assets and inject more than $100 billion in new investment each year into the U.S. market, more than all remittances, direct foreign investment and aid combined that flows from the United States to Latin America. The notion that the U.S. government or the American consumer is subsidizing Latin America and its émigrés is factually wrong. The truth is the reverse—Latin America and its migrants are subsidizing the American way of life, not to mention the U.S. federal government deficit.

The economic impact of illegal immigration in the United States is a debate that has simmered for more than a decade. It is largely accepted that the discounted wages earned by illegal migrants serve to depreciate or freeze the wages of America's lowest-skilled labor. Ostensibly, those lower wages raise the profitability of the labor-intensive industries where they work and provide significant savings to all American consumers when those savings are passed on by business.

Flawed Critiques of Illegal Immigration

In 2004 the Washington-based Center for Immigration Studies published what many regard as the most objective and quantifiable study of the economic costs of illegal immigration. *The High Cost of Cheap Labor Illegal—Immigration and the Federal Budget* provides a detailed analysis of the direct taxes paid and federal budget costs borne by American households headed by illegal immigrants. The study concludes that the average illegal household costs the federal government $2,736 more in federal outlays than it produces by way of direct tax revenue, or in aggregate terms, a $10.4 billion federal tax deficit.

The cost side of the study's analysis is very thorough and includes the attribution of indirect federal costs, such as infrastructure (i.e., road building, ports) and the justice system, to these households. The cost analysis demonstrates that households led by undocumented workers cost the government more than the average U.S. household in food assistance, welfare programs, treatment for uninsured and education, all reflecting the higher number of children born into an undocumented household versus the U.S. average. What the study fails to point out is that a large percentage of those children are U.S. citizens, having been born here, even while their parents are illegal immigrants. Furthermore, those children will grow into tax-paying adults, a vital ingredient in the future viability of the U.S. tax system, given the low birth rates among American-born parents.

Positive Contributions of Illegals

Illegal immigrants . . . positively contribute to the US economy as consumers in the market. Though there have not been significant quantitative estimates of the contribution that illegal immigrants make, it is important to acknowledge their impact. [UCLA political economy professor Raul] Hinojosa estimates that 90 per cent of the wages that the undocumented population earns are currently spent inside the US. As a result, he holds that the total consumptive capacity of illegal immigrants remaining in the US is around $450 billion.

Recent years have also witnessed a marked increase in the use of *matrícula* cards—photo identification cards given out by the Mexican consulate to Mexican nationals; the Mexican government reports that a vast majority of *matrícula* applicants do not have documented status. Nonetheless, these cards are accepted as valid identification by companies such as Sprint, Costco and Wells Fargo, which has, for example, opened 525,000 *matrícula* accounts (6 per cent of the bank's total). Another company—No Borders Inc.—sells debit cards to *matrícula*-holders on which they can store cash and send remittances home. In addition, health insurers like Blue Cross of California have begun to sell health insurance to *matrícula*-holders. The growth in acceptance of *matrícula* demonstrates the growing desire on the part of US businesses to capture the consumer buying power of illegal immigrants.

Ramanujan Nadadur,
Journal of Ethnic and Migration Studies, *July 2009.*

The study goes on to point out that undocumented workers tend to shun many of the federal spending programs such as social security, cash welfare programs, Medicaid and veteran benefits, even while contributing to each.

The most glaring critique of undocumented workers that emerges from the analysis is the fact that they cost the U.S. taxpayer $791 per undocumented household in terms of Immigration and Naturalization Service enforcement, court proceedings and jail time. Most of these costs, however, come from the very enforcement of an outdated and unrealistic immigration policy.

Last but not least, the study presumes that legal households generate a balanced budget, in contrast to the $10.4 billion deficit caused by illegal immigrants. Yet, in 2002, the U.S. federal budget recorded a $158 billion deficit, equal to $1,450 per household.

Even with its obvious flaws in detail, the study fails to address the strongest fiscal and financial arguments in support of the role of immigrant labor, which fall outside the cost side of the tax ledger. The tax revenue contribution attributed to undocumented workers misses the mark precisely because it focuses exclusively on taxes paid by these people, who in large numbers work in the untaxed cash economy. It fails to recognize the additional taxable business profit generated by the discounted wages of 7.2 million productive illegal immigrants or the additional savings to consumers that is spent on taxable goods. Excluding the positive economic impact of lower undocumented migrant wages from the equation is like declaring the 8.1 billion hours of free service by America's 61 million volunteers as economically irrelevant.

Savings Passed on to Americans

Illegal migrants work mostly in the agriculture and construction industries. The National Homebuilders Association reported that in 2002, the average new American home cost

$298,412, of which $68,000 was spent on the labor portion of the house. In a study by Barry Chiswick of the University of Illinois in 2003, he estimated that the 14% of the construction labor force made up of illegal workers provides a $5,000 per household savings to home builders. In 2002, 1.6 million homes were built in the United States, so roughly $8 billion in additional profit was realized by home builders or saved by consumers, equal to 7.3% of the labor cost of U.S. home building (i.e., undocumented construction workers cost employers half the normal rate). In the $118 billion U.S. agriculture industry, illegal immigrants, who make up 24% of the labor force, helped save U.S. farmers and/or consumers approximately $6.8 billion.

Illegal immigrants provide a significant bottom-line impact on many service industries across the country. They represent 15% of the cleaning workforce and 12% of the food preparation workforce but reach as high as 47% of the meatpacking industry and 44% of the horticultural sector. Wherever present, illegal workers push down the cost of menial labor, providing savings to business and consumers. According to the Pew Research Center, America's 7.2 million illegally immigrated workers make up 4.9% of the nation's workforce. Assuming that illegal labor normally works for half of the fully burdened cost of documented workers (including employment taxes and insurance), then their collective work effort generates an estimated $64 billion in savings, the spoils of which are divided between business and consumers. If employers hoard the savings for themselves, they pay an additional $12.9 billion in business taxes to Uncle Sam. If all those savings are passed onto consumers, then every American can thank their Mexican handymen and gardeners, Ecuadorian kitchen staff, Colombian nannies, and Honduran fruit-pickers for approximately $215 per year the hard work of those people saves them.

What these numbers reveal is what hard-working Latino workers have always known—that they contribute far more to the U.S. economy than they cost. . . .

Essential to America's Economy

As U.S. lawmakers struggle to design an immigration policy that functions in the 21st century, they would do well to abandon both the nostalgia of Ellis Island [an early twentieth-century immigration center] and the paranoia of isolationists and instead treat immigration, including illegal immigration, as an integral component of economic globalization. Immigration is vital to a country like the United States where a generation of low birth rates and under-funded math and science education has left the labor pool with holes at the top and bottom. U.S. business needs to import both highly skilled and menial labor in order to compete internationally. Without immigration, our two most competitive industries, information technology and agriculture, will lose market share abroad and jobs at home.

> *"Many illegal immigrants come here precisely because they are criminals and they find America a target-rich environment."*

Illegal Immigration Is Increasing Crime Rates

Roger D. McGrath

Historian and US Marine veteran Roger D. McGrath uses his native Ventura County, California, and neighboring city of Oxnard, California, as case studies in the following viewpoint to make the argument that increases in crime often coincide with illegal immigration. Illegal immigrants, the author notes, commit their first criminal act by crossing the border without the proper documentation. He maintains that these undocumented immigrants often congregate in communities such as Oxnard where the more hardened criminals among them can establish themselves and start up far-reaching drug-dealing enterprises. Within communities of illegal immigrants such as Oxnard, unscrupulous illegal aliens can blend in with the other residents and operate under police radar, as described by the author. McGrath provides specific examples of criminals who have crossed illegally into the United States, often multiple times, only to commit murder and

Roger D. McGrath, "Double Down: Illegal Aliens and Crime," *Chronicles: A Magazine of American Culture*, June 2010. Reprinted by permission.

other serious crimes. This continual disregard for the law, McGrath contends, can only be addressed by deporting all individuals who are in the country illegally, whether they have committed additional crimes after their entry or not.

As you read, consider the following questions:

1. How many of the six "Most Wanted of Ventura County" in the Ventura *Star* newspaper are illegal aliens each week, according to McGrath?

2. As stated by McGrath, how does the murder rate in the city of Oxnard, populated largely by illegal immigrants, compare with the city of Thousand Oaks, populated largely by native citizens?

3. How many inmates charged with Level I crimes have been identified as illegal as part of the Secure Communities Initiative cited by the author?

For too long now I have heard that illegal immigrants are not criminals and that they have come to America only to work. Not really. Whether or not they want to work, they have already committed a crime by illegally entering the United States. I am still naive enough to think that national sovereignty should mean something. Whether or not they want to work, they also come here to have babies. The birthrate for illegal-alien mothers is more than double that for native-born American women, and higher even than the birthrate for legal immigrants. Moreover, the only-want-to-work argument ignores the enormous costs to U.S. taxpayers that come with illegal aliens, especially for medical care and for schooling and other services we provide for their children, American born or not. These costs are helping to sink the city of Los Angeles and the Los Angeles Unified School District in a sea of debt.

As if this isn't bad enough, many illegal immigrants come here precisely because they are criminals and they find America a target-rich environment. This is particularly true of

Mexican criminals, who make a practice of committing crimes in the United States, slipping back into Mexico, and then, rested and equipped with new identities, returning here. I have seen Mexicans deported for their third or fourth time, and each time, the same criminal has a new name. Since this continues to occur with alarming frequency, I am forced to conclude that our southern border remains porous and that our federal officials are not serious about border enforcement.

Evidence of Crimes

My own Ventura County in Southern California suffers from the depredations of such illegal aliens daily. Our local newspaper, the *Star*, prints a weekly feature, "Most Wanted of Ventura County," which includes photos, names, crimes, and full descriptions of the six most-wanted miscreants each week. Week in and week out, four or five of the six, and occasionally six of the six, are Hispanic. Not infrequently, a note will say, "Thought to have fled to Mexico." There are other clues to their illegal-alien status. Their first names are rendered in Spanish rather than in English: There is Timoteo instead of Timothy, Gerardo instead of Gerard, Antonio instead of Anthony, Guillermo instead of William, Rogelio instead of Roger, Diego instead of James. The old-time Mexican-American families in California usually give their children Anglo names. Then, too, many of the miscreants have aliases. Gerardo Rodrigo Lopez is also Rodrigo Ramirez Velasco. An entirely different criminal, Gerardo Garcia Granados, is also Gerardo Rodrigo Lopez. You figure it out. Law enforcement can't.

Late in March [2010], Jose Antonio Medina Arreguin, called the King of Heroin by Mexican authorities, was arrested in the [Mexican] state of Michoacán. For at least the last three or four years he had smuggled an average of 440 pounds of heroin each month into California, earning his organization a monthly gross of $12 million. His distribution center was Oxnard, which is Ventura County's largest and most Hispanic city. One third or more—some say it may be closer to one half—of Oxnard residents are illegal aliens or the children of illegal aliens. Oxnard's crime dwarfs that of every other town in Ventura County. With a population of 180,000, Oxnard usually has 25 or more murders per year. Some 20 miles to the east in Ventura County, Thousand Oaks, with a population of 130,000, largely white and native born, usually has no murders in any given year, although it occasionally sees one or two. Other crime categories reveal similarly striking disparities between the two cities.

Arreguin, or Don Pepe as he was known, found Oxnard ideal for his operations. His gangsters could blend in with the population, move about quite openly, and supply black-tar heroin and methamphetamines to a network of dealers from San Diego to San Jose. Oxnard police and Ventura County sheriff's deputies learned of the operation in 2007 and formed the Ventura County Combined Agency Team. Wiretaps and surveillance led to the first break in 2008 with the arrest of dozens of street dealers and of Don Pepe's drug lords in California—Salvador Alvarez, Julio Ramirez, Jr., and Julio Ramirez, Sr.—and the seizure of 28 pounds of methamphetamines and 131 pounds of heroin. The amount of heroin seized was unprecedented in Ventura County, and yet it represents only a small portion of what Arreguin's organization distributed throughout California each month.

Prosecuting Illegals

Despite intercepting and taping the phone conversations between Arreguin and the Ramirezes, authorities knew Arreguin only as Don Pepe. They eventually determined that he spent most of his time in Michoacán but that the heroin came from poppies grown farther south in the state of Guerrero. The bulk of the heroin was transported to Tijuana and then smuggled across the border in concealed compartments in cars to the distribution center in Oxnard. Agents from the

Drug Enforcement Administration presented the evidence gathered by the Ventura County Combined Agency Team to Mexican authorities, and the latter began their own investigation. After two years of work they finally identified Don Pepe as Arreguin and arrested him in Michoacán's fourth-largest city, Apatzingán. Transported to Mexico City, Don Pepe was paraded in front of reporters, while heavily armed police officers, their faces covered with knit masks and their chests with body armor, stood guard. Arreguin was clearly a big catch.

Ventura County District Attorney Greg Totten is now trying to have Arreguin extradited to Ventura County for trial on various drug-trafficking charges. It could take a year or more to get Arreguin extradited. He may never be. Thus far, Mexican authorities have not revealed whether Don Pepe is a principal figure in La Familia, the powerful drug cartel that dominates Michoacán and has killed hundreds of rival drug traffickers, police, and soldiers. Considering the size of his operation, it would seem that he must have had at least a working relationship with the cartel. I suspect either that serious obstacles will arise to his extradition or that he will not live to be extradited. If he does arrive safe and sound here in Ventura County, his trial will be a sensation.

District Attorney Totten was elated at the success of the Combined Agency Team, saying, "It is the first time that local law enforcement has investigated and prosecuted a drug trafficking organization of this nature that is operating deep within the country of Mexico." Totten's language is a bit paradoxical. Thus far Ventura authorities have only prosecuted the portion of Arreguin's drug-trafficking organization that was operating well within the country of the United States. We haven't penetrated deep into Mexico; Mexican criminals have penetrated deep into the United States. These Mexican gangsters seem to come and go across our border with impunity

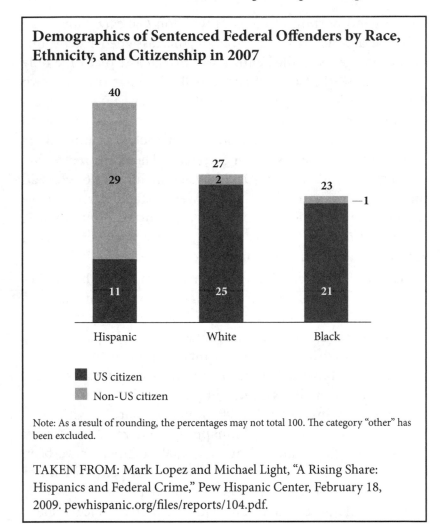

Demographics of Sentenced Federal Offenders by Race, Ethnicity, and Citizenship in 2007

Note: As a result of rounding, the percentages may not total 100. The category "other" has been excluded.

TAKEN FROM: Mark Lopez and Michael Light, "A Rising Share: Hispanics and Federal Crime," Pew Hispanic Center, February 18, 2009. pewhispanic.org/files/reports/104.pdf.

and live openly among other illegal aliens—those who come here "only to work"—in our towns and cities. Why should such conditions prevail?

Number of Illegals in Jails

Until the last few years, most counties made no attempt to determine the immigration status of inmates in their jails. Ventura County was a pioneer in the effort to determine status but only because of the work of the congressman who represents a good portion of the county, Elton Gallegly. More than a decade ago he created a program that assigned federal immigration agents to the Ventura County jail. At that time only two agents worked the jail and usually for no more than two days per week. The agents were able to interview only a portion of the suspected illegal aliens who are arrested and jailed daily. Twenty or thirty were identified each day, but others passed through the system undetected. "There are many that we miss," admitted agent David Wales in July 2006. He said that agents prioritized their interviews, starting with those suspected illegal aliens accused of the most heinous crimes. "There's nothing that is 100 percent, but we work very hard to keep those folks from getting back on the street."

Late in 2008 Gallegly's program was improved by the Secure Communities Initiative, which allows county jails to compare inmates' fingerprints with FBI criminal records and with immigration records maintained by the Department of Homeland Security. The fingerprints housed in the database include only those of people who have had contact with the department. Nonetheless, since implementation of the Secure Communities Initiative, 18,000 inmates, charged with such Level I crimes as murder, kidnapping, and rape, have been identified as illegal aliens. Thus far, 4,000 of them have been deported. Another 25,000 illegal aliens charged with lesser crimes such as burglary have been deported—but that is only a fraction of those incarcerated. Just how many illegal aliens are in our county jails—not prisons—is a matter of speculation, but the figure is conservatively put at more than 100,000.

It is well and good that thousands of illegal aliens who have committed crimes such as murder or rape or burglary have been apprehended and deported, but why did we not stop them at our border in the first place?

Deportees Often Return

Deportation gives the impression that the federal government is finally taking some real action. However, as long as the border remains porous, the illegal-alien felons simply return at their own discretion. For a time I kept a file that eventually ran into the hundreds on local illegal aliens who had been deported multiple times after committing serious felonies. There is now a new crime: committing a felony after previously being deported. It seems unlikely the new law will have much of an effect. Recently, Jose Uriel Zamora was arrested in Santa Paula, once upon a time a quaint Ventura County town that has seen its illegal-alien and gang population multiply several-fold over the last three decades. Zamora was charged with weapons violations, street terrorism, animal cruelty (mistreatment of pit bulls), and committing felonies after previously being deported. I expect to see Zamora tried, convicted, and deported. I also expect to see him back in Santa Paula or some other once-quaint California town before too many years have passed.

One Oxnard resident who was deported and came back to murder (allegedly) is Maximo Tamayo-Flores. A routine traffic stop lcd to Flores's undoing. When a police officer approached the small pickup truck Flores was driving, a woman jumped out screaming. Flores roared off but crashed a short distance away and was arrested after a struggle. Speaking in Spanish, the woman claimed that Flores had murdered her husband, Raymond Quintero Rodriguez, and dumped his body over the side of the Pacific Coast Highway [PCH] north of Ventura. The body was subsequently found on a rocky slope between the PCH and the surf. Flores was immediately charged with assault on a police officer and evading arrest. He was later charged with felony illegal entry into the United States, an offense applied to those who have been deported and have illegally reentered. It is expected that he will also soon be charged with the murder of Rodriguez.

Over the last 30 years I've followed hundreds of similar cases involving illegal aliens in Ventura County—and Ventura County is a relative paradise when compared with Los Angeles

County. None of this has to be. We could deport not only all criminal illegal aliens but all illegal aliens if only we had the political will. That we don't at least deport all illegal aliens who have doubled down by committing crimes—in addition to illegal entry—is especially galling.

> *"Dozens of national studies examining immigration and crime ... all come to the same conclusion: immigrants are more law-abiding than citizens."*

Illegal Immigration Is Not Increasing Crime Rates

Tom Barry

While many studies and voices in the illegal-immigration debate contend that illegal immigrants are the source of increasing crime rates in the United States, Tom Barry argues in the following viewpoint that these claims are just reactionary, fear-mongering exaggerations. Barry contends that numerous studies show that all immigrants, whether legal or illegal, are actually less likely to engage in criminal activities than the native-born US population. Barry blames the current media representation of illegal immigrants as criminals on groups such as the Center for Immigration Studies (CIS) and the Federation for American Immigration Reform (FAIR) that have published scathing condemnations of illegal immigrants. Tom Barry is the senior policy analyst and director of the Center for International Policy's

Tom Barry, "The Truth About Illegal Immigration and Crime: Immigrants, Whether Legal or Illegal, Are Substantially Less Likely to Commit Crimes or to Be Incarcerated than U.S. Citizens," worldhunger.org, February 6, 2008. Reprinted by permission of Tim Barry, Director of TransBorder Project, Center for International Policy.

TransBorder Project, which is dedicated to creating a broader understanding of issues such as immigration, homeland security, and border security.

As you read, consider the following questions:

1. According to statistics cited by Barry, what percentage of Americans believe that immigrants are the cause of increased crime?

2. What are three facts published by the Immigration Policy Center and cited by the author that refute the picture of illegal immigrants as criminals?

3. As stated by Barry, anti-immigration groups such as CIS attribute the underreporting of immigrant crime to what factor?

"Some of the most violent criminals at large today are illegal aliens." That's the lead sentence of a policy report published by the Center for Immigration Studies [CIS], a Washington, DC institute that provides intellectual ammunition to the anti-immigration forces.

Another CIS study led with a similarly impressionistic assertion about the immigrant-crime link: "In recent years, it has become difficult to avoid perceiving immigrants, legal or not, as overwhelming this country with serious crime."

CIS is not alone in relying on impressions to form opinions about just how illegal immigrants are. On the basis of fear-mongering stories rather than scientific studies, groups like the Center for Immigration Studies have succeeded in convincing the media and the U.S. public that undocumented immigrants are criminals. A National Opinion Research Center survey found in 2000 that 73% of Americans believed that immigrants were casually related to more crime.

But, as in other dimensions of the immigration debate, the facts don't support the alarm.

Less Likely to Commit Crimes

There have been dozens of national studies examining immigration and crime, and they all come to the same conclusion: immigrants are more law-abiding than citizens. A 2007 study by the Immigration Policy Center (IPC) found that immigrants, whether legal or illegal, are substantially less likely to commit crimes or to be incarcerated than U.S. citizens.

Ruben G. Rumbaut, coauthor of "The Myth of Immigrant Criminality" study, said: "The misperception that immigrants, especially illegal immigrants, are responsible for higher crime rates is deeply rooted in American public opinion and is sustained by media anecdotes and popular myth." According to Rumbaut, a sociology professor at the University of California at Irvine, "This perception is not supported empirically. In fact, it is refuted by the preponderance of scientific evidence."

The Immigration Policy Center study found that:

- At the same time that immigration—especially undocumented immigration—has reached or surpassed historic highs, crime rates have declined, notably in cities with large numbers of undocumented immigrants, including border cities like El Paso [TX] and San Diego [CA].

- Incarceration rate for native-born men in the 18–39 age group was five times higher than for foreign-born men in the same age group.

- Data from the census and other sources show that for every ethnic group, incarceration rates among young men are lowest for immigrants, even those who are least educated and least acculturated.

As the study noted, the fact that many immigrants enter the country illegally is framed by anti-immigration forces as an assault on the "rule of law," thereby reinforcing the false impression that immigration and criminality are linked.

Recession Has Not Increased Immigrant Crime

The great recession of 2008–09 has obviously reversed some of the national gains against poverty, but the recent growth of the underclass cannot be blamed on low-skilled illegal immigration. According to the Pew Hispanic Center [a research organization], the number of illegal immigrants living in the United States has declined since 2007 as jobs in construction and other sectors where they have traditionally found work have dried up. Fewer are entering the country, and a growing number of them have returned home. Those that remain are far more likely to be working than loitering on street corners. There has been no uptick in crime.

Daniel Griswold, Commentary, *December 2009.*

One of the most disturbing findings of the IPC study was that immigrant children and immigrants with many years in the country are more likely to become criminals than first-generation immigrants or those with less than 15 years in the country. In other words, the more acculturated immigrants are the more likely they are to become criminals—although still at lower rates than those for non-immigrants.

Anti-Immigrant Misinformation

Indignant anti-immigration voices dominate internet discussions with their vitriol and misinformation, and even point to false data to bolster their case.

The anti-immigrant forces draw, for example, on the "2006 (First Quarter) INS [Immigration and Naturalization Service]/ FBI Statistical Report on Undocumented Immigrants" with its array of alarming statistics about illegal immigrants and crime to make their case that undocumented immigrants not only break the law entering the country but also break the laws, with a proclivity to violent crimes, once they make their own homes here. Statistics from this study circulate on restrictionist websites and routinely appear in blogs and post-article comment sections across the web.

In fact, no such report exists. INS, the agency that supposedly produced the report, ceased to exist in 2003.

But facts don't get in the way of those who are intent on demonizing undocumented immigrants or "illegals" in the vocabulary of the restrictionists. How do groups like CIS explain the gap between their impressions and the real statistics about crime and immigration? CIS asks the same question in a 2001 report: Why is it that studies don't make the immigration-crime connection when "so much other evidence indicates they are responsible for a wave of individual and organized crime?"

Contrary to their prevailing argument that immigrant crime is terrorizing the US general public, CIS argues that immigrant crime is unreported because it stays within the immigrant community as immigrant-on-immigrant crime. Furthermore, police departments tend to avoid enforcing laws when immigrants are involved because police are not the agency charged with enforcing immigration law. As Heather Mac Donald argued in a report published by CIS, "In cities where crime from these lawbreakers ['illegal aliens'] is highest, the police cannot use the most obvious tool to apprehend them: their immigration status."

CIS and other restrictionist think tanks argue that given their supposed criminal natures, the best way to solve the crime problem in cities like Los Angeles is to round up the illegal immigrants. "The police should be given the option of reporting and acting on immigration violations, where doing so would contribute to public safety," wrote Mac Donald, a scholar at the conservative Manhattan Institute.

Fear Dominates Debate

Taking off from the findings of studies that immigrant children are more likely to commit crimes than their parents, CIS argues that our society should root out the problem now by deporting the parents of possible future criminals. "On the issue of crime, the biggest impact of immigration is almost certainly yet to come," warns Steve Camarota, director of research at CIS.

The great distance between fact and perception, reality and scenario was all too evident in Iowa and New Hampshire during presidential primaries [in 2008], where fear of immigrants has made immigration a leading campaign issue, especially among Republicans. To hear the candidates and constituents rail against immigration, one would have thought immigrants were flooding across the U.S.-Mexico border on their way to Iowa and New Hampshire.

Stoked by anti-immigration groups like the Federation for American Immigration Reform [FAIR], which publishes alarmist state-by-state profiles of the purported negative impacts of immigrants, restrictionist fever has spread throughout the country. Both Iowa and New Hampshire have overwhelmingly white populations with only a small immigrant population. Even according to FAIR's high estimates, the population of undocumented immigrants or "illegals" does not exceed 55,000 in Iowa and 15,000 in New Hampshire.

Certainly, immigration is an issue that merits public discussion and should be part of the electoral debate. But facts, not irrational fear and dread, should inform the national debate about immigration policy.

> *"It's worse than anybody knows ... [in Arizona border towns]. There are outlaws roaming around with guns, and if you jack with them they'll kill you."*

Illegal Immigration Harms Border Communities

Leo W. Banks

In the viewpoint that follows, Leo W. Banks chronicles the recent rise in crime experienced by US residents of towns bordering Mexico. He argues that citizens in these communities are fed up with the current fear they experience on a daily basis and that those who do not live on the border cannot understand the daily stress and fear border town residents experience. He highlights their dilemma by detailing the recent murder of Arizona rancher Rob Krentz whom authorities believe was killed by a Mexican man who crossed the border illegally and then fled back to Mexico. Banks contends that these types of crimes are up in many small towns along the border as stricter enforcement along other stretches of the border has pushed the illegal entrants toward less-patrolled areas. This shift in crossings, Banks states, has made residents of small border towns fearful for their personal safety, more guarded about protecting their personal prop-

Leo W. Banks, "Cross Country: Our Lawless Mexican Border," *Wall Street Journal*, April 10, 2010. Reprinted by permission.

erty, and more forceful in lobbying their representatives in government to make changes to ensure their security. Leo W. Banks is a journalist who writes about the border situation for Arizona's Tucson Weekly.

As you read, consider the following questions:

1. As stated by Banks, what do most Americans who do not live on the border believe "antipathy toward illegal immigration" arises from?

2. By what percentage did arrests in Douglas, Arizona, rise in 2010, as stated by the author?

3. According to the residents of Douglas cited by Banks, where do National Guard troops need to be stationed and why?

A great sadness will descend over this border town [Douglas, Arizona,] today [April 10, 2010,] as mourners fill the local high school gym to pay their respects to Rob Krentz. Two weeks ago, the 58-year-old rancher was shot and killed by what appears to be a drug smuggler. His death has created a tidal wave of emotion—Krentz was a pillar of this community where his family has ranched land for a century. "The sobbing and crying from people I never thought I'd see cry, it's unbelievable," local veterinarian Gary Thrasher told me.

Residents Live in Fear

Americans who do not live along the Mexican border often assume the antipathy to illegal immigration arises from racial or cultural concerns. But talk to people on the ground, and what they fear most is the loss of personal security. They are angry that the federal government is unable to provide them with this most basic of human rights.

Last year the Border Patrol made an astonishing 241,673 arrests in the Tucson Sector, which covers 262 miles [of the

Arizona-Mexico border]. Arrests in Douglas are up 25% this year—in part because tighter security elsewhere has funneled traffic through this remote region. Border agents say that 17% of the people they arrest in the sector have U.S. criminal records.

On the morning of March 27 Krentz was working on his 35,000-acre ranch when he radioed his brother Phil to say he was in trouble. Krentz's body was found in his Polaris Ranger. Trackers followed the trail of his apparent killer about 20 miles to the border where he crossed into Mexico. As of this writing, the suspect is still at large.

The Krentz ranch sits along the Chiricahua Corridor, a well known smuggling route with dirt trails pounded smooth by decades of foot traffic. For years, Rob's wife, Sue, has written pleading letters to politicians, media and others, detailing how the smuggling of drugs and people has become so bad that family members feared for their lives.

"It's worse than anybody knows," rancher Ed Ashurst told me. "There are outlaws roaming around with guns, and if you jack with them they'll kill you."

Louie and Susan Pope, who live outside the town of Portal [Arizona] some 46 miles from Mexico, lock their valuables in a safe before taking morning horseback rides. They've had three break-ins. According to Susan, the one-room school in Apache where she is a teacher and bus driver has been broken into so often there's nothing left worth stealing. "Americans shouldn't have to live like this," she told me. She is Rob Krentz's sister.

Most illegal immigrants enter the country to work, not to commit serious crimes, and even hard-hit ranchers say some crossers treat property respectfully. But the bad guys are winning. Many of the worst are "southbounders"—coyotes [individuals who smuggle immigrants across the border] who have dropped loads of people or drugs and are heading home. They kick in doors looking for food, water, guns or cash.

Border Residents Want Change

Krentz was a big-hearted guy who was quick to help anyone in need and always calmed people down whenever tempers flared. Now, residents are directing their passions at their political leaders.

At an extraordinary outdoor meeting at the Apache School following Krentz's death, 400 of them gathered in the cold Geronimo wind to press Democratic Rep. Gabrielle Giffords and Republican Senate hopeful J.D. Hayworth for help. In response, Ms. Giffords has written to President Barack Obama and Homeland Security Secretary Janet Napolitano asking for National Guard troops to be sent to the area. Sen. John McCain [Republican senator from Arizona], pressed from the right by Mr. Hayworth, is doing the same.

If the troops come, people in Douglas tell me, they need to be stationed along the border and told to stand their ground. It unnerves them that the Border Patrol often backs far off the line to patrol deep in American territory. This cedes ground to drug runners and gangs. "We're chasing people 10 miles up, 40 miles up, and it's after the fact," Mr. Thrasher told me.

In a Douglas gun shop after the shooting, I watched customers stream in to buy safes and pistols. Even bird-watching ladies from Portal are arming up—they see the threat clearly and understand they face it alone.

The spectacle reminded me of the comment Barack Obama made during the presidential campaign about bitter, small-town Americans clinging to guns and religion. Now his administration is reducing Border Patrol's budget, cutting the number of agents, and denying requests for more vehicles and equipment. The disconnect between Washington's priorities and the border lawlessness creates a sense of abandonment here, leaving many to feel that yes, God and guns are what they have left.

> "Many criminologists say [one Texas border town] isn't safe despite its high proportion of immigrants, it's safe because of them."

Illegal Immigration Does Not Harm Border Communities

Radley Balko

American border towns and their residents often find themselves at the center of debates concerning the impact of illegal immigration on the United States; however, there is much disagreement as to whether these immigrants' presence is beneficial or harmful. In the viewpoint that follows, Radley Balko presents the positive impacts of undocumented immigrants on border towns, countering the view that they are harmful for these communities. Focusing on the low crime rates in cities with high immigrant populations, specifically El Paso, Texas, Balko makes the case that immigrants improve the towns they move to regardless of whether they are documented or undocumented. He maintains that, time and again, border cities with significant numbers of immigrants are ranked among the best cities in the United States to live in and remain open and welcoming to immigrants. Radley Balko is a senior editor of the libertarian magazine Reason.

Radley Balko, "The El Paso Miracle," *Reason*, July 6, 2009. Reprinted by permission.

As you read, consider the following questions:

1. As stated by Balko, how does the number of murders in El Paso, Texas, compare with the number of murders in Baltimore, Maryland?

2. What are the two "happiest" cities in America, according to *Men's Health* magazine, as cited by the author?

3. How has the reception of immigrants in the United States differed from that of immigrants in European countries and changed the way immigrants behave in their new homes, in Balko's opinion?

By conventional wisdom, El Paso, Texas should be one of the scariest cities in America. In 2007, the city's poverty rate was a shade over 27 percent, more than twice the national average. Median household income was $35,600, well below the national average of $48,000. El Paso is three-quarters Hispanic, and more than a quarter of its residents are foreign-born. Given that it's nearly impossible for low-skilled immigrants to work in the United States legitimately, it's safe to say that a significant percentage of El Paso's foreign-born population is living here illegally.

El Paso also has some of the laxer gun control policies of any non-Texan big city in the country, mostly due to gun-friendly state law. And famously, El Paso sits just over the Rio Grande from one of the most violent cities in the western hemisphere, Ciudad Juarez, Mexico, home to a staggering 2,500 homicides in the last 18 months [2008 to July 2009] alone. A city of illegal immigrants with easy access to guns, just across the river from a metropolis ripped apart by brutal drug war violence. Should be a bloodbath, right?

Immigrants Make Border Towns Safe

Here's the surprise: There were just 18 murders in El Paso last year [2008], in a city of 736,000 people. To compare, Baltimore, [Maryland,] with 637,000 residents, had 234 killings. In fact, since the beginning of 2008, there were nearly as many El Pasoans murdered while visiting Juarez (20) than there were murdered in their home town (23).

El Paso is among the safest big cities in America. For the better part of the last decade, only Honolulu has had a lower violent crime rate (El Paso slipped to third last year, behind New York). *Men's Health* magazine recently ranked El Paso the second "happiest" city in America, right after Laredo, Texas— another border town, where the Hispanic population is approaching 95 percent.

So how has this city of poor immigrants become such an anomaly? Actually, it may not be an anomaly at all. Many criminologists say El Paso isn't safe despite its high proportion of immigrants, it's safe *because* of them.

"If you want to find a safe city, first determine the size of the immigrant population," says Jack Levin, a criminologist at Northeastern University in Massachusetts. "If the immigrant community represents a large proportion of the population, you're likely in one of the country's safer cities. San Diego, Laredo, El Paso—these cities are teeming with immigrants, and they're some of the safest places in the country."

If you regularly listen to talk radio, or get your crime news from anti-immigration pundits, all of this may come as a surprise. But it's not to many of those who study crime for a living. As the national immigration debate heated up in 2007, dozens of academics who specialize in the issue sent a letter to then President George W. Bush and congressional leaders with the following point:

Numerous studies by independent researchers and government commissions over the past 100 years repeatedly and consistently have found that, in fact, immigrants are less likely to commit crimes or to be behind bars than are the native-born. This is true for the nation as a whole, as well as for cities with large immigrant populations such as Los Angeles,

Border Town Residents Feel Ties to Both Sides of the Border

As a kid, going back and forth across the [the Rio Grande between El Paso, Texas, and Juárez, Mexico] was no big deal. We did it several times a week—to visit friends and relatives, eat at restaurants, and buy groceries in Juárez. For me the bridge was just a way to get to the other side of a muddy river. . . .

As an adult I still have trouble answering questions at border checkpoints. For some reason interrogations always make me feel guilty. Plus I find it difficult to answer the profound existential questions the customs agents pose at these crossings: Who are you? Where are you from? Where are you going? Why? They're the sort of queries I've never been able to answer truthfully in five hundred words or less. I always simply answer "American" to the citizenship question. But what I really want to say is that I'm a *fronterizo* [borderite]. I'm from both sides.

David Dorado Romo, Texas Monthly, *June 2010.*

New York, Chicago, and Miami, and cities along the U.S.-Mexico border such as San Diego and El Paso.

Immigrants Do Not Commit More Crime

One of the signatories was Rubén G. Rumbaut, a sociologist who studies immigration at the University of California, Irvine. Rumbaut recently presented a paper on immigration and crime to a Washington, D.C. conference sponsored by the Police Foundation. Rumbaut writes via email, "The evidence points overwhelmingly to the same conclusion: Rates of crime and conviction for undocumented immigrants are far below those for the native born, and that is especially the case for violent crimes, including murder."

Opponents of illegal immigration usually do little more than cite andecdotes attempting to link illegal immigration to violent crime. When they do try to use statistics, they come up short. Rep. Steve King (R-Iowa), for example, has perpetuated the popular myth that illegal immigrants murder 12 Americans per day, and kill another 13 by driving drunk. King says his figures come from a Government Accountability Office [GAO] study he requested, which found that about 27 percent of inmates in the federal prison system are non-citizens. Colorado Media Matters [a progressive research and information center] looked into King's claim, and found his methodology lacking. King appears to have conjured his talking point by simply multiplying the annual number of murders and DWI [driving while intoxicated] fatalities in America by 27 percent. Of course, the GAO report only looked at federal prisons, not the state prisons and local jails where most convicted murderers and DWI offenders are kept. The Bureau of Justice Statistics puts the number of non-citizens (including legal immigrants) in state, local, and federal prisons and jails at about 6.4 percent. Of course, even that doesn't mean that non-citizens account for 6.4 percent of murders and DWI fatalities, only 6.4 percent of the overall inmate population.

Border Towns Remain Welcoming

What's happening with Latinos is true of most immigrant groups throughout U.S. history. "Overall, immigrants have a stake in this country, and they recognize it," Northeastern University's Levin says. "They're really an exceptional sort of American. They come here having left their family and friends back home. They come at some cost to themselves in terms of security and social relationships. They are extremely success-oriented, and adjust very well to the competitive circumstances in the United States." Economists Kristin Butcher and

Anne Morrison Piehl argue that the very process of migration tends to select for people with a low potential for criminality.

Despite the high profile of polemicists such as [American radio host and former CNN anchor] Lou Dobbs and [conservative radio host and political commentator] Michael Savage, America has been mostly welcoming to this latest immigration wave. You don't see "Latinos Need Not Apply" or "No Mexicans" signs posted on public buildings the way you did with the Italians and the Irish, two groups who actually *were* disproportionately likely to turn to crime. The implication makes sense: An immigrant group's propensity for criminality may be partly determined by how they're received in their new country.

"Look at Arab-Americans in the Midwest, especially in the Detroit area," Levin says. "The U.S. and Canada have traditionally been very willing to welcome and integrate them. They're a success story, with high average incomes and very little crime. That's not the case in Europe. Countries like France and Germany are openly hostile to Arabs. They marginalize them. And they've seen waves of crime and rioting."

El Paso may be a concentrated affirmation of that theory. In 2007 the *Washington Post* reported on city leaders' wariness of anti-immigration policies coming out of Washington. The city went to court (and lost) in an effort to prevent construction of the border fence within its boundaries, and local officials have resisted federal efforts to enlist local police for immigration enforcement, arguing that it would make illegals less likely to cooperate with police. "Most people in Washington really don't understand life on the border," El Paso Mayor John Cook told the *Post*, "They don't understand our philosophy here that the border joins us together, it doesn't separate us."

Other mayors could learn something from Cook. El Paso's embrace of its immigrants might be a big reason why the low-income border town has remained one of the safest places in the country.

Periodical and Internet Sources Bibliography

The following articles have been selected to supplement the diverse views presented in this chapter.

Daniel Griswold	"Higher Immigration, Lower Crime," *Commentary*, December 2009.
Brian Grow et al.	"Embracing Illegals," *BusinessWeek*, July 18, 2005.
Liz Halloran	"Under the Sun," *U.S. News & World Report*, June 20, 2005.
Miriam Jordan	"Illegal Immigration Enters the Health-Care Debate," *Wall Street Journal*, August 15, 2009.
Philippe Legrain	"Let Them In," *Forbes*, June 28, 2010.
Ruben Navarrette Jr.	"Reformers Can't Ignore Illegal 'Criminal Aliens,'" *USA Today*, March 24, 2010.
Jason Richwine	"A Population Portrait," *National Review*, June 7, 2010.
Walter Rodgers	"Illegal Hispanic Immigration Is Undermining American Values," *Christian Science Monitor*, March 30, 2010.
George F. Will	"Out of What 'Shadows'?" *Newsweek*, June 4, 2007.
Armstrong Williams	"Catering to Illegals," *New York Amsterdam News*, November 1, 2007.

**OPPOSING
VIEWPOINTS®
SERIES**

 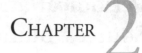

CHAPTER 2

How Should America Enforce Its Borders?

Chapter Preface

On April 23, 2010, the same day governor Jan Brewer signed the Arizona Immigration Bill (SB 1070), which requires immigrants to carry immigration documents in case of police arrest or questioning, President Barack Obama spoke to a crowd attending a naturalization ceremony at the White House to condemn the legislation. The Arizona law and other efforts like it, Obama said, "threaten to undermine basic notions of fairness that we cherish as Americans, as well as the trust between police and our communities that is so crucial to keeping us safe." For Obama, though, the passage of SB 1070 signaled that states were taking extreme measures to counteract the infiltration of America's southern border. In a move some commentators thought was perhaps designed to placate conservative lawmakers, Obama placed twelve hundred National Guard troops along the border in May 2010 to assist US Border Patrol agents with surveillance and anti–drug trafficking programs. Arizona's two US senators, John McCain and Jon Kyl, applauded the president's move, but Kyl lamented to FoxNews.com on May 25 that the National Guard forces were given desk jobs and not patrol duties. "They'll be investigating, administrative support, maybe training," Kyl said. "Now that's all fine . . . but the real value of the National Guard is to be seen."

Three months later, President Obama signed the Southwest Border Security Bill, which earmarked $600 million to bolster current measures to end human smuggling and drug trade in the region. In a brief statement issued on August 12, the president claimed that "the resources made available through this legislation will build upon our successful efforts to protect communities along the Southwest border and across the country. And this new law will also strengthen our partnership with Mexico in targeting the gangs and criminal organizations that operate on both sides of our shared border." The president made no mention of the increased number of Border Patrol agents and aerial drones funded through the bill to monitor and deter border crossings.

Safeguarding the US border has gone hand in hand with stemming illegal immigration. The 1,951-mile-long border fence (actually composed of several barriers spanning parts of Texas, Arizona, New Mexico, and California) was designed to divert drug traffickers and illegal immigrants from gaining easy passage into urban areas along the border. According to a March 2010 survey by the conservative polling organization Rasmussen Reports, 49 percent of Americans favor the expansion of the barrier to halt the drug trade, while 39 percent believe the fence should be expanded to thwart illegal immigration. Few politicians, however, wish to divorce the issues. Governor Brewer made a controversial claim in June 2010, asserting that "the majority of the illegal trespassers that are coming into the state of Arizona are under the direction and control of organized drug cartels." Such claims make it easy to characterize all illegal immigrants as tools of criminals if not always criminals themselves. Critics charge that these blanket portrayals are erroneous and mask discrimination. Alex Di-Branco, writing for immigrant rights at Change.org, insists that "fear-mongering about 'criminal aliens' is just a smoke-screen for the nativism and xenophobia that makes [conservative Americans] support draconian immigration laws and derail comprehensive immigration reform that has a shot at creating a just and enforceable system." In DiBranco's view, most illegal aliens are trying to gain access to jobs to support their families and start new lives in the United States.

In the following chapter, various commentators offer their ideas about how and why the border should be protected. Some believe stringent measures are needed to protect America and make sure its public services are not drained by a growing tide of immigrants. Others fear that tighter enforcement will lead to human tragedies inflicted upon innocent people who simply want a chance to work for a better life.

"The main solution to our illegal immigration problem begins with controlling the border."

Strengthening the US-Mexico Border Is Essential to Stopping Illegal Immigration

Jeff Lukens

One of the most controversial topics in US border security is the building of a fence between the United States and Mexico to stem the tide of illegal immigration. Proponents of the fence contend that the installation of a physical barrier between the two countries is the first, most important step in addressing the problems associated with illegal immigration. Without a fence to stop the flow of immigrants, they maintain that other programs addressing issues such as employment and identification, such as E-verify or the REAL ID Act, will be ineffectual. Jeff Lukens elucidates this argument in the following viewpoint. He contends that current immigration from Mexico to the United States differs from immigration in the past, both in the ease with which immigrants enter the country and their lack of interest in assimilating. He argues that due to these differences illegal immigration today is a problem that requires tougher solutions,

Jeff Lukens, "Just Finish the Dang Fence," *American Thinker*, June 2, 2010. Reprinted with permission.

namely the building of a border fence. Jeff Lukens is a conservative columnist who has written about issues ranging from immigration to the war against terrorism.

As you read, consider the following questions:

1. According to Senator Jim DeMint's statement quoted by Lukens, how long is the border fence supposed to be according to the legislation passed in 2006, and how much has been completed?

2. As stated by the author, who does Mexico "export" to the United States and why?

3. What problems does Lukens highlight with the use of National Guard troops as a border security measure?

Why did building the fence along our southern border stop? Instead of building the fence, [President] Barack Obama would rather build a political party of illegal aliens and their supporters. Unless we want to be dealing with immigration problems in perpetuity, the fence must be completed.

In a recent commentary, Sen. Jim DeMint [a Republican from South Carolina] reported,

Four years ago [in 2006], legislation to build 700-miles of double-layer border fence along the Southern border was supported by then-Sen. Barack Obama and signed into law by President [George W.] Bush. Yet, only a fraction of that fencing is in place today.

According to staff at the Department of Homeland Security (DHS), only 34.3 miles double-layer fencing has been completed along the Southern border.

The lack of double-layer fencing can be traced to a 2007 amendment that eliminated the double-fencing requirement and allowed the DHS the option to put other types of less effective fencing in its place. It was lumped into a massive, omnibus-spending bill that President Bush signed into law on December 26, 2007.

But since President Obama took office [in January 2009], construction on the fence has halted. Apparently the solution then was to use a "virtual fence" by way of drones and sensors. DeMint goes on to say U.S. Customs and Border Patrol Chief Alan Bersin dashed any hopes left for the virtual fence when he called it a "complete failure" during a recent Senate hearing.

The New Immigrants from Mexico

Almost everyone supports legal immigration, where we gradually assimilate newcomers into the population. No previous group, however, has had such a large inflow or ease of access to their home country as Mexican immigrants have today. That's because no previous wave of immigrants could walk right into the country. Earlier groups crossed oceans to come here and were assimilated into the culture in a measured way.

The income gap between the U.S. and Mexico is the largest between any two neighboring countries in the world. The Mexican economy does not provide living wages for its growing population, and their solution is to export their poor to our country.

Most Americans clearly want the federal government to get tougher on illegal immigration. While politicians pander for cheap labor and cheap votes, we the taxpayers pick up the tab for their emergency room visits, education, and other social services. When we factor in the increased taxpayer expense and the fraying of the social fabric of our nation, cheap labor is not so cheap after all.

Moreover, today's illegals do not conduct themselves like immigrants of the past. Certainly, many are hard workers. However, they are here against our laws and have little or no

US Southwestern Border Patrol Sectors and Location of the Border Fence and SBInet

— State boundary

Border Patrol sector

■ Fence completed
(Data source: OBP)

▌ Fence under construction
(Data source: USACE)

▌ Fence planned/under contract
(Data source: USACE)

○ SBInet [virtual fence—
networked cameras and radar]

Note: The depiction of the fence was derived from various digital database sources. US Customs and Border Protection assumes no responsibility or liability for any errors or omissions. Fence depiction is not to scale. The map is conceptual and does not depict the actual size of the fence.

TAKEN FROM: Chuck McCutcheon, "Securing Our Borders: Doing What Works to Ensure Immigration Reform Is Complete and Comprehensive," Center for American Progress, April 2010. www.americanprogress.org.

interest in learning English or the ways of our culture. Illegals generally come here to find a job, not necessarily to become citizens.

And now they are protesting our generosity in the streets while Mexican President Felipe Calderón denounces Arizona's enforcement of federal law to standing ovations in Congress. While Washington plays politics with border security, the politicians' inaction is leading to increased drug trafficking, human trafficking, and gang activity in the border states.

These brazen attitudes and behaviors are offensive to Americans, and they are why we need the border controlled. This is not about racism. It is about an abuse of our laws and social norms that appalls every ethnic group, especially those waiting in line legally to become citizens.

Border Fence a Permanent Solution

So far, all efforts to secure the border have failed. Calling up National Guard troops is only a stopgap measure. The Guardsmen will eventually go home. Whatever funding provided this year for border protection may be cut next year, and then we could be right back where we started. We need something tangible. A fence is permanent, and we need to build it.

Other actions need to be taken to control illegal immigration such as a foolproof, biometric identity card for employment and stiff penalties against companies who hire undocumented workers. But those actions can wait. The main solution to our illegal immigration problem begins with controlling the border, and controlling the border starts with building a fence. Sen. DeMint's efforts to finish the fence should be applauded.

Once a fence is in place and we restore order on the border, our ability to handle guest worker programs and related issues becomes possible. Only when the border is truly secure will Americans trust Washington to pass a comprehensive immigration system that works.

We have a proud history of accepting the world's poor in a system designed to provide gradual assimilation of new citizens into our language and culture. We need to control our border and allow that process to happen properly.

| "No wall, moat or border patrol will be large or wide or deep enough to fully stop the flow of immigrants."

Strengthening the US-Mexico Border Will Not Stop Illegal Immigration

Peter Schrag

Many proponents of increased border security believe that building a wall on the southwestern border of the United States as well as increasing border patrol are two essential steps to halting illegal immigrants as they try to enter the country. Opponents of increased border security like Peter Schrag, however, contend that strengthening the border leads to unintended consequences and distracts attention from the real problems with current immigration policy that encourages illegal immigration. In the viewpoint that follows, Schrag attributes the increase in number of illegal immigrants not to lax border enforcement, but to tightened border controls that discourage workers from returning to Mexico upon the expiration of visas and consequently encourages them to bring their families into the United States. Schrag suggests alternative methods to combat increased illegal immigration resulting from both these policies and globalization, an-

Peter Schrag, "Why Strengthening the U.S.-Mexican Border Leads to More Illegal Immigration," *Washington Post*, July 18, 2010.

other factor he sees as a catalyst for the current influx of immigrants. Peter Schrag is a columnist and the author of Not Fit for Our Society: Immigration and Nativism in America.

As you read, consider the following questions:

1. As stated by Schrag, what is the total cost of border security annually?

2. What is the driver of immigration, according to the author?

3. What are some of the strategies that Schrag suggests the United States employ to combat illegal immigration?

Even before 2007, when the last attempt at comprehensive immigration reform was killed in the Senate, immigration restrictionists made "sealing" the U.S.-Mexican border a precondition for supporting legalization of the more than 11 million illegal immigrants already in the United States. For a lot of Americans, this idea has been orthodoxy ever since.

Now, with immigration reform again on the table, President [Barack] Obama has duly taken up the call for a stronger border. In his speech on immigration earlier this month [July 2010], he lamented the "porous" and "broken" state of U.S. borders, and he described controlling them as an "obligation" and a "responsibility," arguing that the nation has "more boots on the ground near the Southwest border than at any time in our history."

More than 670 miles of border fences, walls, bollards and spikes that Congress decreed in 2006 at an estimated cost of $4 billion (plus future maintenance) are almost completed. The Border Patrol, which was increased from 9,000 agents in 2001 to 20,000 in 2009, costs an estimated $4 billion annually.

Throw in the cost of occasional deployments of the National Guard, as Obama has ordered again; the cost of electronic sensors, surveillance aircraft, training of local police; the cost of detaining, incarcerating and deporting illegal immigrants; and the countless other expenses associated with border security, and the bill runs us nearly $10 billion a year.

Unintended Consequences

But will more boots really seal the border? Immigration reform has a long history of unintended consequences: More than two decades of increased enforcement since the passage of the Immigration Reform and Control Act [IRCA] of 1986[1] has done little to reduce the number of illegal immigrants. In fact, it seems to have increased their numbers. Meanwhile, the question of jobs, which are the true driver of legal and illegal immigration, has been largely neglected.

Princeton University sociologist Douglas Massey pointed out nearly a decade ago that measures to secure the border seemed to produce almost the opposite of what was intended. By making the northward crossing more dangerous and expensive, Massey and co-authors Jorge Durand and Nolan J. Malone wrote in 2002, the border buildup discouraged seasonal laborers from going back to Mexico when they were not working.

With increasing border enforcement, workers who used to shuttle between jobs in California or Texas and home in Zacatecas or Michoacán simply began to stay put and sent for their families, becoming permanent, if sometimes reluctant, residents. According to Massey, post-IRCA border enforcement may have increased the size of the permanent Mexican population in the United States by a factor of nearly four.

More unintended consequences: The anti-immigrant backlash that sparked Arizona's string of anti-immigration legislation—the new law[2] seeking to drive illegal immigrants out of

1. The Immigration Reform and Control Act of 1986 made it illegal to knowingly employ an illegal immigrant, increased border security, and allowed for the legalization of some immigrants already living in the United States.
2. Arizona's Senate Bill 1070, signed into law on April 23, 2010, requires police officers to check the immigration status of those stopped for possible legal infractions if the police officers believe them to be in the country illegally. It also requires that all immigrants carry their immigration papers. As of January 2011, the law's constitutionality was still under judicial review.

Border Fence Will Harm Wildlife

The remote, unforgiving, staggeringly diverse country that straddles the border between Arizona and the Mexican state of Sonora is one of the most politicized landscapes in the world, a place long caught up in the ferocious international debate over immigration. Solid fences and other barriers are now expanding along the entire southwestern border.... Largely forgotten in these plans, however, are the jaguar, the chronically endangered Sonoran pronghorn—now making a tenuous U.S. recovery in southwestern Arizona—and scores of lesser-known creatures. While barricades reach into the wild country of southern Arizona and beyond, these species await the consequences.

"If the wall goes up, it will be a complete and absolute barrier for terrestrial wildlife," says Christine Hass, assistant director of the Audubon Appleton-Whittell Research Ranch, in Elgin, Arizona, and a wildlife ecologist who has studied carnivores in the region for more than a decade. "It has the potential to have more impact here than anything we've ever seen."

Michelle Nijhuis,
Audubon, *September/October 2007.*

the state most famously among them—was produced in large part by tighter border controls in Texas and California. That enforcement squeezed the smuggling of immigrants and drugs into Arizona's Sonoran Desert and mountains.

Economy Drives Immigration

As noted by the nonpartisan Public Policy Institute of California among many others, the element missing from this picture is that immigration, both legal and illegal, is driven more by the economy than it is restrained by border enforcement.

That's not all that different from the immigration patterns of the past century and a half, when immigration levels were almost invariably trailing indicators of the U.S. economy and its sometimes severe worker shortages. One hundred fifty years ago, after the dislocations and slaughter of the Civil War, some states even sent agents to Europe to recruit workers. When times were good, we beckoned to immigrants; when they were bad, we tried to expel them. "We wanted workers," says Philip Martin, an immigration economist in California, "but we got people."

Americans have historically been ambivalent about new arrivals. Ever since colonial days, immigration and immigration restriction have been tightly wound around each other like a double helix. In the same polls in which Americans express support for Arizona's immigration legislation, they also say that by paying fines and back taxes (which most already pay) immigrants should have the right to be legalized. Some places accept, even welcome, illegal immigrants. Some try to expel them. My own state of California grants illegal immigrants relatively low in-state college tuition but denies them driver's licenses.

In the past three years, the U.S. population of illegal immigrants has declined, perhaps by as much as 10 percent, from about 12 million to 11 million. Anti-immigration groups such as the Center for Immigration Studies credit tougher border and workplace enforcement for much of that decline. But some, if not most, has almost certainly been driven by the recession, beginning in the construction industry and continuing in many other sectors that employ large numbers of immigrants. During those three years, more immigrants returned to Mexico than came north.

None of this means giving up on border control, especially if it's focused on drugs and other criminal activities. But if the objective is to reduce the attraction of U.S. jobs for undocumented workers—about a third to half of whom, in any case, have overstayed their visas, not crossed the border illegally—it requires different strategies.

New Strategies

In the past year, the federal Immigration and Customs Enforcement agency has conducted "silent raids"—auditing farms and businesses to check employee records and then, using the threat of large fines, forcing them to fire illegal immigrants. But given the dependence of tens of thousands of employers on such workers—about 60 percent of U.S. farm workers are believed to be undocumented—it's hard to imagine that quiet raids will be enough to drive out many of those 11 million illegal immigrants.

Probably the most promising workplace strategy, which has hardly been tried, would be far more rigorous enforcement of labor laws on wages, hours and overtime, and of worker safety laws. That would sharply reduce employer incentives to hire and exploit illegal immigrants. In a small step in that direction this summer [2010], Labor Secretary Hilda Solis moved to crack down on the employment of young children in agriculture. But that's barely a start.

For the long term, immigration scholars such as Robert Pastor of American University argue that in order to deter illegal immigration we should shift funding from ever-tighter border control to collaborative efforts to bolster Mexican infrastructure and economic development. He cites the economic aid the European Union provided to Spain and Portugal when it admitted those countries in 1986: This aid seems to have effectively reversed the flow of immigrants from those nations to the rest of Western Europe.

The best way to pursue such a strategy, Pastor argues, would be to create something he calls "the North American Community." This body, which would include Canada, the

United States and Mexico, would manage a range of matters, from crime control, drugs and continental security to transportation, the environment and labor.

The Changing Nature of the Border

But for the millions who cross between the United States and Mexico every day to work, study and shop, and for those involved in thousands of joint commercial and cultural institutions, the border is already more a region than a line. Thus, in many ways what Pastor proposes via formal institutions already exists on the ground.

"Our two largest trading partners are not England and China," he pointed out in 2007, "but Canada and Mexico. The two largest sources of energy imports are not Saudi Arabia and Venezuela, but Canada and Mexico. . . . There are roughly 500 million legal crossings of both borders each year, and the preferred tourist destination of Canadians, Mexicans and Americans is their neighbors in North America."

Given the world's integrated economy, and the rapidly changing nature of, and constraints on, the nation-state—think terrorism, or the flow of illegal drugs, or the regulation of multinational corporations, or the Internet, or pollution—no wall, moat or border patrol will be large or wide or deep enough to fully stop the flow of immigrants.

Trying to tightly seal any border will almost inevitably bring unintended consequences—in reluctant illegal residents, in increased offshoring of industry and jobs, in cross-border smuggling and crime or, as with Arizona's new immigration law, in a whole new set of foreign policy problems.

"Show me a 50-foot wall," Homeland Security Secretary Janet Napolitano said when she was governor of Arizona, "and I'll show you a 51-foot ladder."

> "Programs like 287(g) help restore rule of law by removing those individuals who break the law and enter the U.S. illegally."

Program 287(g) Has Helped State and Local Law Enforcement Fight Illegal Immigration

Jena Baker McNeill

While the securing of US borders and the enforcing of immigration law have historically fallen to federal agencies, the recent increased flow of illegal immigrants into the United States has led US Immigration and Customs Enforcement (ICE) to enlist the aid of state and local law enforcement through programs such as 287(g). Under such programs, the federal government provides training, resources, and funding to local agencies to aid in the enforcement of immigration policy. In the viewpoint that follows, Jena Baker McNeill applauds these efforts and argues that recent reports criticizing such programs as ineffectual and leading to racial profiling are inaccurate. To highlight her contentions, McNeill presents the findings of a recent report published by the

Jena Baker McNeill, "Section 287(g): State and Local Immigration Enforcement Efforts Are Working," Heritage Web Memo 2405, April 22, 2009. Reprinted by permission.

Davidson County, Tennessee, sheriff's office praising the program and its success within the community. She goes on to call for the extension and continued support of these programs by the federal government. Jena Baker McNeill is an international studies and homeland security policy analyst at the conservative public policy think tank the Heritage Foundation.

As you read, consider the following questions:

1. Before local law enforcement officers can act as ICE agents, what must they undergo, as stated by McNeill?

2. According to the Davidson County Sheriff's Office report cited by the author, how many illegal aliens has the office arrested and processed for removal in the two years since the implementation of 287(g)?

3. What are the benefits of 287(g) as highlighted by Mc-Neill?

State and local law enforcement across the country have begun to tackle their jurisdictions' illegal immigration woes. One such program, Section 287(g), allows Immigration and Customs Enforcement (ICE) to train state and local police to enforce federal immigration laws.

The Government Accountability Office (GAO), however, claimed in a March [2009] report that the programs were unorganized and a source of racial profiling. But a report by the Davidson County (TN) Sheriff's Office provides a very different take, emphasizing that 287(g) is highly valuable.

Congress should continue its support for 287(g) and other state and local ICE programs by allocating more funding to ICE ACCESS programs like 287(g) and Department of Homeland Security (DHS) resources. It should simultaneously make it easier for state and local governments to use homeland security grants to pay for program participation. Finally, it should ensure that program progress is reported to Congress annually.

Empowering Local Law Enforcement

ICE and state and local law enforcement have long struggled to enforce America's immigration laws. Previously, when a state and local law enforcement officer apprehended an individual who could not demonstrate legal presence in the U.S., the officer would simply notify ICE and wait for them to come and get the individual. In practice, this meant many illegal aliens went free and immigration laws were not enforced.

In 1996, however, Congress created 287(g) programs as an amendment to the Immigration and Nationality Act (INA). ICE now offers a full menu of immigration-enforcement-related assistance programs for state and local law enforcement called ICE ACCESS.

These programs allow DHS to enter into Memorandums of Agreement with state and local law enforcement. In the case of 287(g), this status allows law enforcement entities to "act in the stead of ICE agents by processing illegal aliens for removal." Before officers can take such steps, however, they are required to undergo a five-week training course, a background check, and mandatory certifications. There are currently 29 jurisdictions around the U.S. participating in 287(g) programs.

287(g) Is a Success in Tennessee

On March 4, [2009,] the GAO issued a report that was highly critical of 287(g) programs, including accusations that 287(g) was poorly run, lacked oversight, and could lead to racial profiling. While the report used no statistics to confirm that profiling was occurring, the charges managed to ignite a firestorm of criticism at House hearings on the issue.

A recent report by the Davidson County Sheriff's office, however, paints a different picture of 287(g) programs. The Sheriff's Office has reportedly arrested and processed for removal over 5,300 illegal aliens in two years (many with current or previous criminal charges). These efforts have also led

Local Police Tackle Illegal Immigration

Though the government seems to avoid keeping statistics on illegal-immigrant crime, there's more than anecdotal evidence that illegal immigrants are responsible for a great deal of crime. Prince William County in Virginia is part of a federal program to fund and train state and local law-enforcement departments to enforce immigration laws. Known as the 287(g) program, it has drawn wide interest from across the country. Since July of 2007, Prince William County has issued over 1,600 detainers under the initiative. From 2007 to 2008, according to the 2008 crime statistics for the county, violent crime plunged 21.8 percent. Over the last two years, violent crime has dropped by almost 37 percent in the county. Other areas of Virginia have seen rates remain stagnant or even increase. The neighboring county witnessed a dramatic upwards spike.

"Of course, our unique policy on criminal illegal aliens is clearly producing results," explained Corey Stewart, the chairman of the board of county supervisors. . . . "Our innovative policy on criminal illegal aliens has drawn a lot of attention, and with the eyes of the world upon them, there has not been one substantiated claim of racial profiling or intolerance among our sworn officers."

Alex Newman, New American, *July 20, 2009.*

to a 31 percent decline in arrests of "foreign-born" individuals and a 46 percent decline in "illegal aliens committing crimes."

The report also addressed the racial profiling issue detailed in the GAO report. Davidson County emphasized that the individuals removed through 287(g) did not disproportionately affect a particular race, as those arrested represented 61 different countries of origin.

Furthermore, as the percentage of foreign-born individuals arrested in the county has decreased 31 percent since the program's inception, there is nothing to support a claim of racial profiling. In fact, Davidson County emphasized that it had never received allegations of profiling and had engaged in extensive community communication efforts to decrease concerns.

Benefits of 287(g)

As evidenced in the Davidson County report, ICE ACCESS programs, including 287(g), have the following benefits:

- *They help fight crime.* Using ICE databases, 287(g) participants can identify serious criminals and arrest and remove them from the United States. For example, Davidson County was able to get 90 gang leaders off the streets through its 287(g) efforts.

- *They are effective in removing illegal immigrants.* There are approximately 11 million illegal immigrants in the United States. These individuals often strain government services, placing a particularly large burden on state and local governments, who often end up footing the bill. Programs like 287(g) help restore rule of law by removing those individuals who break the law and enter the U.S. illegally.

- *They respect federalism.* State and local governments have the right to enforce federal laws or enact and enforce their own laws. And the Tenth Amendment's concept of federalism leaves areas unregulated by federal or state law to the people. As long as state and local governments operate within the parameters of the Constitution and federal law, their sovereign authority to look after their citizens is not in question.

Support and Expand Programs

The Davidson County report emphasizes why 287(g) programs work and why they should be continued. Similar success stories have been highlighted by many jurisdictions around the country. For instance, the sheriff of Frederick County, Maryland, relayed similar positive benefits from its 287(g) program in the March [2009] congressional hearings.

Congress should recognize the success of 287(g) and other ICE ACCESS programs and do the following:

- *Maintain support for ICE ACCESS programs.* Congress should ensure that these programs continue. Doing so recognizes the constitutional ability of the states to enforce federal immigration laws, decreasing both crime and illegal immigration, while protecting the U.S. border.

- *Require more communication to Congress.* Congress should require DHS to brief them on ICE ACCESS programs annually. This will give Congress an opportunity to exercise oversight over the progress, ask questions, and receive feedback from the program.

- *Allocate more resources to participants.* GAO officials cited a shortage of resources as a reason behind the perceived lack of organization/oversight of 287(g). Congress should fully fund these ICE ACCESS programs and expand them. For example, DHS could allow states and cities to use homeland security grants to pay for their participation, including overtime costs for state and local law enforcement agents assisting in immigration enforcement investigations.

Congress should recognize the valuable role that state and local law enforcement can and do play in keeping America safe, combating illegal immigration, and protecting the nation's borders—and encourage the growth and expansion of 287(g) and other similar programs.

> *"In the 66 local police departments that participate in the 287(g) program, there is evidence that actual crime-fighting is suffering because of the focus on immigration enforcement."*

Program 287(g) Has Harmed Local Law Enforcement's Crime-Fighting Focus

Ann Friedman

The contentious Immigration and Customs Enforcement program known as 287(g) was created to allow local law enforcement officials to perform the duties of federal immigration officers in an effort to combat illegal immigration. Opponents of the program see its implementation as encouraging racial profiling by the officers who are a part of it and distracting from serious crime-fighting efforts. In the viewpoint that follows, Ann Friedman takes this stance and argues that in localities where law enforcement participates in 287(g), community security has deteriorated as a result of officers' increased focus on deporting illegal immigrants, oftentimes for minor infractions. She focuses specifically on the actions of Arizona's Maricopa County sheriff Joe Arpaio, whose controversial actions have led to national

Ann Friedman, "Nativism Versus Security," *American Prospect*, September 10, 2009. Reprinted by permission.

criticism of the program. Ann Friedman is the deputy editor of the liberal magazine the American Prospect.

As you read, consider the following questions:

1. In how many of the sixty-six departments participating in 287(g) does Friedman say there is evidence that "actual crime-fighting" has suffered?

2. As stated by the author, what message does 287(g) send to Hispanic communities?

3. What is the new requirement in 287(g) designed to do, according to Friedman?

It's tempting to write off Maricopa County [Arizona] Sheriff Joe Arpaio as just another right-wing hatemonger. Like the Pat Buchanans and Lou Dobbs of the world, he has a large platform, talent for exploiting the racist side of populism, and an all-consuming desire for attention.

So what sets Arpaio apart? Whether we like it or not, he's more than a blowhard. His Arizona county covers 9,000 square miles. It has a population of nearly 4 million. He has 4,000 employees and 3,000 "volunteer posse" members. And although his tactics are under investigation by the Justice Department, he continues to receive financial support from the [Barack] Obama administration.

Jeopardizing Security

When it comes to his actions on immigration, the federal policy that empowers him is the 287(g) provision, which essentially allows local police and sheriffs to act as national-security officials. This "partnership" with the office of Immigration and Customs Enforcement (ICE) has enabled Arpaio to turn his law-enforcement bureau into a racial-profiling and immigrant-hunting unit. ICE brags that, through 287(g), local police have identified more than 100,000 "potentially removable aliens."

Limitations of the 287(g) Program

Removing aliens who have committed violent crimes is of great importance to the safety of the community at large. Through the 287(g) program and its partnerships with state and local agencies, ICE [Immigration and Customs Enforcement] has an opportunity to identify and train additional law enforcement resources that could help it meet this challenge. However, the lack of internal controls governing the program limits ICE's ability to take full advantage of this additional resource. For example, without documenting that the objective of the program is to remove aliens who have committed serious crimes or pose a threat to public safety, participating agencies may further burden limited detention resources by continuing to seek ICE assistance for aliens detained for minor crimes. According to ICE, it is important to ensure that their limited detention bed space is available for those aliens posing the greatest threat to the public. Moreover, without consistently communicating to participating agencies how and under what circumstances 287(g) authority is to be used, participating agencies may use this authority in a manner that is not intended by ICE. Additionally, given the rapid growth of the program, the lack of defined supervision activities could hamper ICE's ability to ensure management directives are being carried out appropriately. . . . Finally, performance measures are important to provide ICE with a basis for determining whether the program is achieving its intended results.

US Government Accountability Office, January 2009.

But in the 66 local police departments that participate in the 287(g) program, there is evidence that actual crime-fighting is suffering because of the focus on immigration enforcement. Several prominent police chiefs have called for 287(g) to be repealed. Not only does the program push them to investigate the citizenship status of every person who appears to be Hispanic, it deters undocumented immigrants from reaching out to authorities when they are victims of or witnesses to crime. Police officers' core mission may be to ensure public safety, but 287(g) sends the message that the mission doesn't extend to Hispanics. "How can you police a community that will not talk to you?" one participating police chief asks, in a report on 287(g) by the Police Foundation. And since all the time spent checking documents is time not spent on other law-enforcement priorities, everybody loses—not just the Hispanics who are profiled.

ICE officials have said the program is designed to target "serious criminal activity." But a Government Accountability Office [GAO] report on 287(g) released earlier this year [2009] found that in more than half of the 29 jurisdictions it investigated, officers expressed concerns that 287(g) was being used to deport immigrants who had only committed minor crimes, such as traffic violations. Along with local advocacy groups, it called on the federal government to amend the program.

Enabling Racial Profiling

Perhaps in response to the GAO's call for stricter regulation of 287(g) partners, in July [2009], Homeland Security Secretary Janet Napolitano announced changes to the program that were decried both as an expansion of the program (by immigrant-rights advocates) and a limitation of it (by deportation hawks). ICE added another 11 jurisdictions to its list of partners and also a requirement that police pursue all charges on which they detain immigrants, a change designed to deter them from deporting those with minor infractions. "This new agreement supports local efforts to protect public safety by giving law enforcement the tools to identify and remove dangerous criminal aliens," Napolitano said.

She should know better. As the former governor of Arizona, Napolitano and Arpaio go way back. Arpaio, one of the most popular politicians in the state, gave Napolitano a boost when he endorsed her 2002 run for governor. And for most of her time in office, she looked the other way as he overstepped his bounds. During her final months as governor, she diverted some state funds from his office, but she never spoke out against his tactics.

In the best possible scenario—the one that ICE touts in its press release—287(g) would merely enable local police to conduct screenings at jails to determine if those already in custody for serious crimes are undocumented immigrants. But Arpaio's actions are a glimpse of how 287(g), in practice, often leads to racial profiling, rather than deportation of dangerous criminals. A recent *New Yorker* profile of Arpaio describes him conducting raids on towns with a high percentage of Hispanic residents. And his chief of enforcement bragged to *The New York Times* last year [2008] that most deputies in Maricopa "can make a quick recognition on somebody's accent, [or] how they're dressed."

The 287(g) program pushes those who are on the margins of our society even further out. But even if Napolitano doesn't care about the rights of Hispanics—or, in Maricopa at least, brown-skinned people wearing clothing styles common in Mexico—she should care about the crime ignored as cops conduct immigration sweeps. As long as Napolitano allows ICE to continue its partnership with jurisdictions like Arpaio's, she's jeopardizing the very security she's supposed to protect.

> *"Arguments we hear today about [the deportation of millions of illegal immigrants] being logistically impossible are nothing more than a mask concealing a lack of political will."*

Deporting All Illegal Immigrants in the United States Is Possible

Roger D. McGrath

While much of the debate about illegal immigration deals with methods of deterring illegal immigrants from entering the country, determining what to do with the illegal immigrants already living in the United States is another crucial concern. Mass deportation is one proposal that has been hotly contested for years. While opponents of this solution contend that it is a' nearly impossible undertaking, proponents, like Roger D. McGrath, argue that it is not logistically impossible but that the government and people today lack the political will to implement the deportation policies necessary to make such a plan successful. In the following viewpoint, McGrath presents a historical account of the mass deportation carried out by Immigration and Naturalization Service commissioner Joe Swing in 1954 to prove that such a policy

Roger D. McGrath, "Deporting Illegal Immigrants," *New American*, July 13, 2010. Reprinted by permission.

can lead to a dramatic reduction in illegal immigrants living in the country. McGrath contends that if politicians today took the same action, such mass deportations would be possible again. Roger D. McGrath is an historian and US Marine veteran.

As you read, consider the following questions:

1. As stated by McGrath, what was the total number of illegal immigrants sent back to Mexico as a result of Commissioner Joe Swing's operation in 1954?

2. How many INS agents did Swing have in the field at any one time, according to the author?

3. What agency does McGrath blame for the ineffectiveness of deportation operations today?

Pardon me, but if I hear one more time that we can't deport 12 million illegal aliens I'm headed for the backyard to howl at the moon. Is the American memory so short that we've already forgotten the 1950s? This writer is old enough to remember very clearly the mass deportation of illegal aliens that occurred in 1954 in what was officially termed "Operation Wetback" (prior to the age of political correctness).[1]

Anyone living in Southern California then, even a kid like me, couldn't help but take notice of the operation that sent upward of two million illegal aliens from all across the Southwest home to Mexico. It was done swiftly and cheaply by a relatively small force, proving that arguments we hear today about such an operation being logistically impossible are nothing more than a mask concealing a lack of political will.

First Invasion of Illegal Immigrants

During World War II, with so many Americans in the service—and fighting and dying overseas—Mexicans illegally entered the United States to take advantage of employment op-

---

1. The word *wetback* has been in use since at least the 1920s as an often derogatory term for illegal Mexican immigrants, who usually had to enter the United States by swimming or wading through the Rio Grande.

portunities, especially as agricultural laborers. People seem to forget that most of those who worked in the farm fields of California during the 1930s were not Mexicans but "Okies," a term applied collectively to the hundreds of thousands of migrants who poured out of not only Oklahoma but also Texas, Arkansas, and Missouri—and smaller numbers from Kansas and Colorado—and took Route 66 to the Golden State. By 1940, the Okies constituted about 12 percent of California's population overall, 25 percent of the population of the agricultural San Joaquin Valley, and the bulk of farm labor. Following the Japanese sneak attack on Pearl Harbor, though, the Okies began moving from the fields into the factories or the Armed Forces.

By the end of World War II, there were some two million illegal aliens living in California, Arizona, and Texas. U.S. citizens in those states began complaining that the Mexican illegals undercut the workingman's wages, committed crimes, caused a general deterioration of the communities they lived in, gave birth to children at county expense, and sent older children to local schools—crowding classrooms and breaking school district budgets. It took years for the complaints of U.S. citizens to gain any traction.

Corruption and Lobbying Efforts

There was already an unholy alliance of agribusiness and other employers of unskilled labor and Congressmen. Corporate farmers and other business interests argued that the work performed by illegal aliens was desperately needed. However, several studies, including one conducted by the President's Commission on Migratory Labor in Texas, demonstrated that if employers paid standard American wages there would be plenty of Americans able and willing to take the jobs. In the Rio Grande Valley of Texas, for example, where tens of thousands of illegal aliens were employed, wages were half that paid in other parts of Texas for the same agricultural jobs.

Lyndon Johnson, a Congressman from Texas at the time, first as a Representative and later as a Senator, fought vigorously against measures aimed at illegal aliens and was said to have been in the hip pocket of agribusiness. He was not alone. While American citizens throughout the Southwest complained about the presence of illegal aliens in their communities, Congress was generally unresponsive. Agribusiness had well-paid lobbyists and influence peddlers by the dozen. American citizens suffering from illegal aliens had no such advocates.

It took a military man, who thought that national borders should mean something, to take action. Even before he was elected President during the fall of 1952, Dwight Eisenhower was concerned about illegal aliens. In 1951, in a letter to Senator William Fulbright of Arkansas, who had recently proposed that Congress create a special commission to examine the influence of lobbyists and unethical conduct by government officials, Eisenhower quoted a line from an article in the *New York Times* that said, "The rise in illegal border-crossing by Mexican 'wetbacks' to a current rate of more than 1,000,000 cases a year has been accompanied by a curious relaxation in ethical standards extending all the way from the farmer-exploiters of this contraband labor to the highest levels of the Federal Government."

It seems that corruption was a fact of life in the Immigration and Naturalization Service [INS] and in the Border Patrol. Herbert Brownell, Jr., Eisenhower's first Attorney General, said that America "was faced with a breakdown in law enforcement on a very large scale. When I say large scale, I mean hundreds of thousands were coming in from Mexico without restraint." They were also staying here without restraint. Border Patrol agents tell stories of rounding up illegal aliens on large farms, only to have them released after the politically connected employer called the right people.

Eisenhower Takes Action

Once firmly established in the White House, Eisenhower went to work on the problem. Early in 1954, he appointed retired Lt. Gen. Joseph "Jumpin' Joe" Swing as the new Commissioner of the INS. Eisenhower could not have made a better choice. Handsome and square-jawed with sparkling blue eyes, white hair, and a bearing that suggested strength and decisiveness, the 60-year-old Swing could have come from Central Casting. The New Jersey–born Swing had been a classmate of Eisenhower at West Point [the US Army academy], graduating in 1915 as a member of "the class the stars fell on."

Fresh out of the academy, Swing participated in the Punitive Expedition against [Mexican revolutionary] Pancho Villa, who raided the border town of Columbus, New Mexico. Swing rose to captain during World War I but remained stateside. He was a full bird colonel by the time World War II erupted and fought in the New Guinea, Leyte, and Luzon campaigns. He landed on Leyte as a major general and commander of the 11th Airborne Division—the "Angels"—which fought brilliantly throughout the Philippines. Included among its feats were the destruction of the vaunted [Japanese] *Shimbu* force, the spectacular rescue of more than 2,000 Allied prisoners behind enemy lines at Los Baños [an internment camp in the Philippines], and a combined parachute and glider operation at Aparri that trapped a Japanese division, leading to its annihilation. Jumpin' Joe was in the thick of things and by war's end his decorations included the Distinguished Service Cross (second only to the Medal of Honor), the Distinguished Service Medal, three Silver Stars, the Legion of Merit, three Bronze Stars, and two Air Medals.

Mass Deportation Begins

With such a background, it is not surprising that Swing provided aggressive leadership as Commissioner of the INS, reorganizing the service and appointing fellow retired generals to key posts. Corrupt and powerful Congressmen, such as Senator Lyndon Johnson of Texas who served the interests of corporate agribusiness and had been able to frustrate the efforts of the Border Patrol, now found themselves facing a new kind of Commissioner in Swing. Moreover, Swing had the full support of President Eisenhower. Disregarding political pressure from Johnson and other such Congressmen, Swing quickly formulated a plan for the apprehension and deportation of illegal aliens, naming it Operation Wetback. On D-day, June 17, 1954, Swing sent 750 of his Border Patrol agents into the field to begin a sweep through Arizona and California. Within a month, Jumpin' Joe's boys had taken more than 50,000 illegal aliens into custody—and half a million more, fearing arrest, had self-deported.

During the second half of July, teams of agents were sweeping through Utah, Nevada, and Idaho. They also went into Texas, targeting especially the Rio Grande Valley. Starting at the valley's southern end and supported by local law enforcement, Border Patrol agents moved northward. On the first day of the sweep, July 15, they took nearly 5,000 illegal aliens into custody. Although not many more than 700 agents were in the field, Border Patrol officials exaggerated the numbers to frighten illegal aliens to flee south of the border. Newspaper editorials, hostile to the operation and in support of corporate interests, also exaggerated the numbers of agents to give the impression that a federal invading army had descended upon the valley. Whether from these exaggerated reports or from actual arrests of illegal aliens, the "wetbacks" of the valley were crossing the border back into Mexico on their own by the thousands each day. The process of self-deportation, demonstrated daily in large numbers during Operation Wetback, is left unmentioned by those who argue that mass deportation of illegal aliens is logistically impossible.

Those taken into custody by the Border Patrol—about 1,100 a day after big numbers during the first week—were transported across the border in trucks and buses and then put on trains bound for Durango. The United States wanted the illegal aliens shipped deep into Mexico to discourage re-entry. They were also taken to Port Isabel, Texas, and put aboard ships such as *Emancipation*, which then sailed them to Veracruz, 500 miles to the south. Transportation by sea continued until seven illegal aliens jumped off *Mercurio* in an escape attempt and drowned. Since the United States depended upon the cooperation of the Mexican government in sending illegal aliens deep into Mexico's interior, protests from Mexico over the drownings caused the United States to end water-borne deportations.

Operation Wetback's Success

By the end of September, the INS estimated that nearly 100,000 illegal aliens had been taken into custody in Texas and deported and that another 700,000 or so [had] self-deported. Adding those to the numbers of illegal aliens deported or self-deported from Arizona and California, and still more from Utah, Nevada, and Idaho, means that in a few months of aggressive patrolling Jumpin' Joe's agents had directly or indirectly sent more than 1.3 million illegal aliens back to Mexico. Moreover, Swing had accomplished this with not many more than 700 agents in the field at any one time and limited funding. What he did have in abundance was the determination and will to enforce the law. For the rest of Swing's tenure as Commissioner, which ended in 1961, illegal border crossings were down 95 percent. The aggressive and common-sensical approach in policing the border that Jumpin' Joe established continued to have a salutary effect on border conditions until the mid-1960s when the rate of illegal crossings began increasing dramatically. There were many reasons for the sudden increase, but it's beyond coincidental that by that time Lyndon Johnson had become President.

During his years as Commissioner, Swing came in for criticism from all the likely sources, including Congressmen who were connected hip-to-hip with agribusiness and other employers of cheap (to the employers only) Mexican labor. Swing, who had "a hair trigger temper" but also a great sense of humor, did not suffer fools or corrupt politicians gladly and simply responded matter-of-factly, and thus politically incorrectly, to the problems caused by the presence of illegal aliens and slack border security. He also liked to emphasize that while special interests might have a problem with him, the great majority of American people wholeheartedly supported Operation Wetback and his strict border policies. Also, supporting Swing was the American G.I. Forum, an organization of Mexican-American military veterans. Together with the Texas State Federation of Labor, the G.I. Forum published *What Price Wetbacks?*, a study which demonstrated that not only did illegal aliens undercut wages and displace American workers but that the de facto open-border policy of past years was a threat to the security of the United States. Most members of Congress also supported Swing, voting in 1958 to increase his salary as Commissioner of the INS from $17,500 a year to $20,000.

Political Will Is Absent

What Swing did in 1954, we could do today—if we had the political will. Retired Border Patrol agent Walt Edwards, who participated in the sweep through the Southwest in 1954, declared in 2006, "Some say we cannot send 12 million illegals now in the United States back where they came from. Of course we can!" Edwards also noted, "When we start enforcing the law, these various businesses are, on their own, going to replace their [illegal] workforce with a legal workforce." Donald Coppock, who was also with the Border Patrol during the 1950s and led it from 1960 to 1973, said that if Eisenhower were President and Swing Commissioner today, they'd seal the border and deport illegal aliens "in a minute."

Another Operation Wetback, though, would also require the abolition of a little-known but byzantine [archaic] and powerful agency within the Department of Justice formally termed the Executive Office for Immigration Review and commonly referred to as the EOIR. The agency was created in 1983 through an internal DOJ [Department of Justice] reorganization, essentially establishing Immigration Courts independent of the INS. Since then immigration attorneys on behalf of their clients have flooded the EOIR with endless paperwork, postponements, and appeals, which can drag what should be a quick and incontestable deportation into years of delays. Moreover, Immigration Court decisions can be appealed to the Board of Immigration Appeals [BIA] and decisions of the BIA can be appealed to a federal circuit appellate court. Summary deportation that prevailed in 1954 has been replaced by infinite immigration litigation. During these proceedings most illegal aliens are released on an immigration bond. If an illegal alien sees that his case is going badly and he will be ordered deported, he simply fails to appear for his final hearing. There are more than 300,000 illegal aliens in such a status.

Strong Leaders Needed

In its report, *The Deportation Abyss: It Ain't Over 'Til the Alien Wins*, the Center for Immigration Studies reports:

> Between the incompetence of the INS [now ICE], the complete lack of alien detention center space, and the bureaucracy of the EOIR, our system for deporting known illegal aliens and criminal alien residents is a sad joke. But no one is laughing.

> If all of the illegal aliens and deportable resident alien criminals were rounded up tomorrow, the system would not be capable of handling them. It would be an absolute disaster. The INS and EOIR wouldn't have the foggiest idea of what to do with them! The aliens would all be released back out

on the street on immigration bonds and go back right where they were as if nothing happened, while their cases would grind on through the system of Immigration Court hearings and endless appeals.

The creation of the EOIR, like the creation of most federal bureaucracies, in turn spawned an entire industry. There are now thousands of attorneys who specialize in immigration law. They are represented by their own lobbying group, the American Immigration Lawyers Association (AILA). Meanwhile, the EOIR employs more than 200 immigration judges, all pulling down six-figure salaries and enjoying generous federal benefits, a far cry from Commissioner Swing's top salary of $20,000.

We got ourselves into this mess and we can get ourselves out of it. However, to do so it will take bold, decisive, and forceful leaders the caliber of Lt. Gen. Joseph Swing—that is if America still produces such men.

| "The federal price tag to deport all undocumented immigrants currently in the United States is prohibitive."

Deporting All Illegal Immigrants in the United States Is Unrealistic

Marshall Fitz, Gebe Martinez, and Madura Wijewardena

With the population of illegal immigrants in the United States ranging from an estimated 10 to 12 million, many politicians and pundits have begun calling for a mass deportation program to expel all these individuals from the country. Opponents of this solution, such as the authors of the following viewpoint, argue that the cost alone of this type of program makes it an impractical solution to deal with the population of illegal immigrants. Marshall Fitz, Gebe Martinez, and Madura Wijewardena's calculations of the expenditure necessary to deport the illegal immigrants from the United States is based on the costs to complete tasks in four areas—apprehension, detention, legal processing, and transportation—and the continuing output necessary for five years after the completion of the initial program to maintain low levels of illegal immigrants. They estimate the total cost of

Marshall Fitz, Gebe Martinez, and Madura Wijewardena, "The Costs of Mass Deportation: Impractical, Expensive, and Ineffective," Center for American Progress, March 2010. Reprinted by permission.

mass deportation to be $285 billion, a figure they contend makes the program infeasible. Marshall Fitz is the director of immigration policy at the Center for American Progress (CAP), a liberal public-policy think tank. Gebe Martinez is a senior writer and policy analyst at CAP. Madura Wijewardena is a lawyer from Sydney, Australia, who became involved in American politics during the 2008 presidential elections, campaigning for Barack Obama.

As you read, consider the following questions:

1. As calculated by the authors, what is the average cost per person to apprehend an illegal immigrant in the United States?

2. What ongoing tasks would the federal government be responsible for after the completion of the deportation program, according to the authors?

3. What is deportation through attrition, as stated by the authors?

While policymakers from across the political spectrum agree that our immigration system is broken, there continues to be debate over whether mass deportation and sealing off the U.S.-Mexico border is a viable, sensible solution. This [viewpoint] breaks down the costs of a mass deportation program—that is, how much it would cost the federal government to expel all undocumented immigrants who are currently in the United States.

Using available data from the increased immigration enforcement activities of recent years, this calculation drew on the Department of Homeland Security's actual spending levels for FY [fiscal year] 2008 and on its estimates of current [as of March 2010] undocumented immigration levels to reach the total cost of around $200 billion. The number of people targeted for removal is based on the total number of undocumented immigrants in the country. . . .

Mass Deportation by the Numbers

While there is evidence that the Great Recession [which began in late 2008] and improved security measures slowed down the influx of undocumented immigrants, the net number of undocumented immigrants in the United States has remained fairly stable. The Department of Homeland Security [DHS] reports that the undocumented immigrant population increased by 300,000 between January 2005 and January 2009 to the current total of 10.8 million.

The DHS figure of 10.8 million undocumented immigrants equals 3.5 percent of the national population of 309 million. This is nearly the same as the population of Georgia and close to the number of everyone living in New England. But casting a dragnet nationwide would obviously be infinitely more difficult than closing the borders of a single state or region of the country.

There are four major tasks that would be essential to conducting the kind of mass deportation and removal process advocated by anti-immigration hardliners in the United States.

- *Apprehension*—Arresting all undocumented immigrants currently in the United States

- *Detention*—Holding in custody (or supervising the interim release of) those who have been apprehended until their cases are heard and legal deportation orders are issued by the relevant legal authority

- *Legal processing*—Adjudicating, under the relevant legal authorities, those who have been apprehended and detained

- *Transportation*—Ensuring that those who have been issued removal orders depart the United States

Let's consider the costs of each of these tasks in turn.

The Costs of Apprehension

The first and most important cost driver for a government deportation policy is locating and arresting as many of the undocumented people in the United States as possible. The cost of apprehension varies widely depending on the location and circumstances surrounding each case, as well as the length of time an undocumented immigrant has lived in the country. Locating day laborers in border cities, for example, is significantly easier than identifying people who are more deeply embedded in communities farther away from the border.

The increasing size and scope of worksite arrests over the past several years, however, makes cost projections somewhat more tangible and underscores the likelihood that a deportation campaign would trigger massive costs. In one enforcement operation in May 2008, the federal government spent $5.2 million—from preparation to follow-up costs—on a raid at the Agriprocessors Inc. slaughterhouse in Postville, Iowa, which led to the detention of 389 mostly undocumented immigrant workers.

To calculate the cost of apprehending 8.64 million undocumented immigrants we use U.S. Immigration and Customs Enforcement, or ICE, appropriations and arrests data from FY 2008. ICE's total budget for apprehension-related expenditures, including salaries but excluding capital projects, totaled $1.24 billion. That figure was divided by the number of arrests recorded—67,728—in order to arrive at a per person average cost of $18,310 per apprehension. The average cost per person was then multiplied by the 8.64 million undocumented immigrants to be apprehended. That resulted in nearly $158 billion in estimated costs for apprehensions. . . .

The Costs of Detention

The responsibility for managing detention of undocumented immigrants rests with ICE. The 32,000 beds currently available under the detention system lack direct federal oversight and management. They are spread out across 350 facilities operated by county governments or private contractors that are mostly designed for penal, not civil detention.

There also are 15,300 spaces for a program testing alternatives to detention using community-based supervision strategies. As the operator of the largest detention and supervised release program in the country, ICE's responsibilities are enormous. In FY 2008, there were 378,582 foreigners from 221 countries in custody or in programs supervised by ICE at various times.

Given the large number of detentions in jail spaces operated by various jurisdictions, ICE has had difficulty managing the workload. There have been more than 100 documented deaths since October 2003, as well as numerous cases of abuse. Alleged violators of civil codes in immigration law are frequently imprisoned in facilities that were designed for offenders of more serious and violent crimes.

In addition, access to legal counsel is uneven at best, and information about problems within the detention system has been suppressed. While DHS has made a concerted effort to start correcting the issues, its overwhelming caseload has prevented it from making rapid progress on reforms.

The estimated funding required to detain 8.64 million undocumented immigrants from the time of apprehension until the time of removal involved determining the average daily cost to detain a noncitizen ($111.82) and the average number of days (30) that an individual in removal proceedings is detained. That per person detention cost was then multiplied by the 8.64 million undocumented immigrants to arrive at an estimated cost of approximately $29 billion.

For purposes of transparency and consistency in these overall calculations, we assume ICE will not build additional facilities to handle the extra demand for detention space, but will continue its current policy to rent it from private contractors and local governments. Were ICE to build its own facilities, as it would almost certainly need to under this strategy, the costs of detention would be far higher.

The total incarcerated population for the United States in 2008 was 2.4 million prisoners. That included all inmates held in local, state, federal (including ICE), military, and juvenile facilities in the United States, U.S. territories, and Indian tribal lands. A deportation strategy that would take place over five years would add an additional 1.73 million inmates to those rolls, a 71 percent increase in the jail population, in each of those five years. In other words, private or public construction of new facilities would be inevitable.

Nonetheless, because of the difficulty in projecting the capital costs of such a strategy and in the interest of adopting conservative assumptions in making these calculations, we rely on the known average detention costs under the current system. . . .

The Costs of Legal Processing

The legal processing costs to the federal government we calculate . . . are the amounts required to process 8.64 million undocumented immigrants through the immigration courts after they have been apprehended. This [viewpoint] only covers the cost of adjudications, not prosecutions. The cost of prosecutions, which are carried out by ICE's Office of the Principal Legal Advisor, were included in the apprehension costs.

Legal processing of apprehended undocumented immigrants is undertaken by immigration courts that are part of the Executive Office of Immigration Review [EOIR] in the U.S. Department of Justice. EOIR has around 230 immigration judges in more than 50 immigration courts around the country. In removal proceedings, immigration judges determine whether an individual from a foreign country should be allowed to remain in the United States or be deported.

As with other areas of the deportation process, immigration courts are structurally flawed and severely ill equipped to serve the current caseload. It is difficult to fathom how the immigration legal system would handle 8.64 million new adjudications that would come from a deportation campaign. The current system's failings were extensively documented in a February 2010 report prepared for the American Bar Association's Commission on Immigration.

Among the report's recommendations are an immediate restructuring to make the immigration courts independent of politics or any administrative agency, and the immediate hiring of 100 new judges plus necessary law clerks to handle the surge in cases stemming from current enforcement policies. These recommendations did not take into account any mass deportation strategy. In 2008, there were 291,781 legal proceedings for undocumented immigrants, or just over 3 percent of the 8.64 million cases necessary to complete a mass deportation.

To calculate the legal processing costs for EOIR of a mass deportation, we identified the FY 2008 appropriations dedicated to the processing of undocumented immigrants, which was $238.32 million. That was applied to the 291,781 legal proceedings for undocumented immigrants to arrive at an average cost of $817 for each legal proceeding. The average was then multiplied by 8.64 million undocumented immigrants for a total legal processing cost of more than $7 billion. . . .

The Cost of Transportation

Undocumented immigrants who have been apprehended, detained, and then legally processed must be moved out of the United States to complete the deportation process. Transportation costs include surface and air transportation to deport undocumented immigrants to their source countries.

The vast majority of individuals who would be put into removal proceedings would eventually require transport out of the country, but some would be eligible for and would accept a "voluntary departure order." That legal mechanism provides the immigrant more flexibility and time to prepare to move from the country but requires them to pay their own way.

In FY 2008, around 28 percent of removals were accomplished through voluntary departure orders. These orders are issued to certain undocumented immigrants who, after being arrested, are determined to satisfy certain legal criteria and who elect to voluntarily return to their home country within a short period. That allows the U.S. government to avoid picking up the transportation tab. We assume a similar percentage of the processed population will receive voluntary departure under a deportation program and accordingly, we reduce the population requiring government transportation by an additional 28 percent. We estimate that the total population who will require government transport is *6.22 million.*

The transportation of 6.22 million undocumented immigrants under a deportation scenario would be a massive undertaking because they arrive in the United States from all over the world.

Currently, U.S. Immigration and Customs Enforcement and U.S. Customs and Border Protection [CBP] have different programs for transporting undocumented immigrants. Most undocumented immigrants from Mexico who are apprehended at the border by CBP are bused across the border. Other undocumented immigrants are transported by plane.

During FY 2008, ICE's Detention and Removal Operations Flight Operations Unit in partnership with the Justice Prisoner and Alien Transportation System transported almost 200,000 undocumented immigrants. This program operated seven charters outside of the Americas, returning 495 alien passengers to Albania, Cambodia, Egypt, Indonesia, Jordan, Morocco, Nigeria, Pakistan, Philippines, Palestinian Authority, and Liberia. In FY 2008, this program had an appropriation of $135 million.

Additionally, ICE and CBP have transportation programs for certain categories of undocumented immigrants. The Interior Repatriation Program transports undocumented immigrants into the interior of Mexico. This program is available for noncriminal Mexican nationals with final orders of removal, processed by CBP for expedited removal, and deemed "at risk" from falling victim to heat or border criminals due to age, physical condition, or travel status. In FY 2008, 49,793 people were removed under this program.

Despite the different countries of origin of undocumented immigrants, and the various methods and programs of repatriation, little public information is available on actual costs to transport the average detainee out of the United States. During congressional testimony in 2007, however, ICE Assistant Secretary Julie Myers estimated a $1,000 per person average transportation cost for deportees.

The Office of the Federal Detention Trustee also reported a per person transportation cost for federal detainees, including deportees, of $999 in FY 2008, and projected a $1,190 per person cost in FY 2011. For purposes of this [viewpoint], the cost was rounded out to $1,000. That means the total cost to transport 6.22 million people overseas at $1,000 apiece equals more than $6 billion.

Total Deportation Costs

The sum of the funding required to apprehend, detain, legally process, and expel 8.64 million individuals out of the United States is $200 billion.

If a mass deportation strategy were seriously pursued, it is safe to assume that it would be a multiyear endeavor. For purposes of evaluating the direct costs of such a strategy in context, we presume this would entail a five-year process at a minimum.

All of the costs set forth in the sections above are conservatively calculated one-time projected costs to identify and remove almost every undocumented immigrant in the United States. Even if that specific objective were practically accomplishable, achieving it would not eliminate the federal government's continuing immigration enforcement mandate during and beyond the mass deportation period.

Continuing Enforcement Costs

The federal government will remain saddled during (and beyond) the five-year mass deportation effort with the ongoing massive expenditures associated with:

- Securing our land borders, coastlines, and ports of entry

- Identifying and removing those who still arrive illegally

- Tracking and removing individuals who overstay their visa, violate the terms of their admission, or commit crimes.

The expenditures on border and interior immigration enforcement have burgeoned since FY 2005. The U.S. Customs and Border Protection and Immigration and Customs Enforcement budgets increased by nearly 80 percent to $17.1 billion in FY 2010, from $9.5 billion in FY 2005. And yet the net undocumented population still slightly increased over that time from 10.5 million to 10.8 million, with the most significant drop in population occurring after the start of the Great Recession in December 2007.

Practically speaking, that means that while the federal government was doubling down on enforcement efforts over a five-year period, it wasn't even able to halt growth in the size of the undocumented immigrant population. In other words, the current ICE and CBP budgets (plus a massive recession) were almost sufficient to prevent a net increase in undocumented immigrants but insufficient to diminish it. As such, in addition to the massive infusion of new resources documented above that would be needed for the discrete task of removing all of today's undocumented immigrants, the federal government would need to spend at or above current levels just in order to prevent a new wave of undocumented immigrants from arriving in the country.

To ensure sufficient border and interior resources to prevent new entries, apprehend those who make it through, and identify and remove those who overstay their lawful visas or violate their status, the ICE and CBP budget outlays would, at a minimum, need to remain constant. Congress appropriated $11.4 billion for U.S. Customs and Border Protection and $5.7 billion for Immigration and Customs Enforcement in FY 2010, for a total of $17.1 billion. Adjusting that amount to 2008 dollars so that it is consistent with the cost of deportation calculations, we arrive at a continuing annual cost of around $17 billion.

Of course, it is true that the ICE and CBP budgets include more than immigration enforcement resources. But it is also true that the capital and infrastructural costs needed to maintain and support contraband smuggling interdiction efforts, for example, cannot be cleanly divorced from human smuggling interdiction costs. In addition, not included in this budget calculation are significant immigration enforcement costs borne by other DHS entities such as U.S. Citizenship and Immigration Services [USCIS]. Costs related to two important USCIS programs, E-verify and US-VISIT, are not reflected in this estimate.

The practical reality is that we will need to maintain the entire ICE and CBP budgets at the very least in order to retain current enforcement levels over this deportation period and beyond. If anything, we believe this understates the actual ongoing enforcement costs that will be required to maintain the status quo.

As such, on top of the $200 billion cost of removing all current undocumented immigrants, the government would be required to expend an additional $85 billion ($17 billion per year for five years) over that same five-year period. Hence, the sum of the five-year immigration enforcement costs under a mass deportation strategy comes to a grand total of $285 billion.

Seeking Sensible Solutions

The undeniable conclusion ... is that the federal price tag to deport all undocumented immigrants currently in the United States is prohibitive. The operational feasibility of such a massive effort is dubious at best. It would require an unprecedented deployment of resources, and the problems currently plaguing our detention system and immigration courts would be exacerbated in the extreme and would likely precipitate widespread human rights and due process violations.

Moreover, a mass deportation strategy would have a crippling impact on economic growth. The exorbitant direct costs of such a strategy ... should be the final nail in the coffin of a moribund idea.

Notwithstanding the fact that some members of Congress and many other advocates are actually calling for mass deportation, some immigration restrictionists complain that the argument against mass deportation is a straw man [where the opposition's position is misrepresented]. These individuals claim that their proposal is more humane and less costly and they call it deportation through attrition: make life hard enough for undocumented workers through heavy-handed enforcement that people simply pack their bags and leave the country.

It should be absolutely clear, however, that the attrition strategy is nothing more than a thinly veiled variation on mass deportation. The basic premise of this idea is that the United States can and should implement a national policy that will drive nearly 11 million undocumented immigrants and millions more of their U.S. family members out of the country. The devastating economic impact and crushing fiscal burden of such a strategy would be indistinguishable from the mass deportation proposal.

It is time to heed the public's call for tough, fair, and practical solutions with a comprehensive immigration reform program that treats immigration as a national resource to be managed and embraced.

| "SB 1070 simply codifies federal law into state law and removes excuses and concerns about states' inherent authority to enforce these laws."

Arizona's SB 1070 Immigration Law Simply Codifies Federal Law into State Law

Russell Pearce

In April 2010, the state of Arizona passed SB 1070, illegal immigration legislation designed to help state and local law enforcement apprehend illegal immigrants. Immediately after its passage, protests resounded nationwide decrying the legislation as racist and an intrusion on individual civil rights. Champions of the act, like Arizona Republican state senator Russell Pearce, who sponsored the bill through its passage, maintain that the law only helps to enforce existing federal law and protect American citizens. In the viewpoint that follows, Pearce explains his support for SB 1070 and argues that the bill has already had a positive impact on his state because it has driven illegal immigrants from Arizona to neighboring states. The state senator re-

Russell Pearce, "Arizona or San Francisco: Which Path on Immigration?" *Human Events*, May 17, 2010. Reprinted by permission.

futes claims that the law is racist, stating that instead it simply provides law enforcement officials with the ability to inquire about an individual's citizenship when they come into contact with them as the result of "normal 'lawful conduct.'" Russell Pearce was elected to the Arizona state senate in 2009.

As you read, consider the following questions:

1. Pearce claims that he proposed SB 1070 for what reasons?

2. As stated by the author, when do states have "inherent authority to enforce immigration laws"?

3. What evidence does Pearce present to support his claim that SB 1070 is "already working"?

I am Arizona State Sen. Russell Pearce, the author of SB 1070 [Arizona's illegal immigration act], which was signed by Gov. Jan Brewer. Fear mongering and misinformation is the tool of the left against this common-sense legislation.

Paul Kantner of the 1960s rock band Jefferson Airplane once remarked, "San Francisco is 49 square miles surrounded by reality." When I first heard that San Francisco was planning to boycott Arizona over SB 1070, this description seemed apt.

However, when the neighboring Oakland City Council voted 7-0 to boycott Arizona last week [May 2, 2010], and President Pro Tem of the California State Senate Darrell Steinberg announced a campaign in the legislature to also boycott the state, it became clear that San Francisco is merely ahead of the California crazy curve.

Federal Law into State Law

Why did I propose SB 1070? I saw the enormous fiscal and social costs that illegal immigration was imposing on my state. I saw Americans out of work, hospitals and schools overflowing, and budgets strained. Most disturbingly, I saw my fellow citizens victimized by illegal-alien criminals.

The murder of Robert Krentz—whose family had been ranching in Arizona since 1907—by illegal-alien drug dealers was the final straw for many Arizonans. But there are dozens of other citizens of our state who have been murdered by illegal aliens. Currently 95 illegal aliens are in Maricopa County jail for murder. When do we stand up for Americans and the rule of law? If not now, when? We are a nation of laws, a constitutional republic.

Most of the hysterical critics of the bill do not even know what is in it. SB 1070 simply codifies federal law into state law and removes excuses and concerns about states' inherent authority to enforce these laws and removes all illegal "sanctuary" policies. The law does not allow police to stop suspected illegal aliens unless they have already come across them through normal "lawful conduct" such as a traffic stop, and explicitly prohibits racial profiling. Illegal is not a race, it is a crime.

Aside from the unfounded accusation of racial profiling, the chief complaint about the bill is that it infringes on federal jurisdiction by enforcing laws. Arizona did not make illegal, illegal. It is a crime to enter or remain in the U.S. in violation of federal law. States have had inherent authority to enforce immigration laws when the federal government has failed or refused to do so.

For all their newfound respect for the authority of federal immigration law, the open-borders advocates who oppose SB 1070 have no problems with "sanctuary cities" across the country that explicitly obstruct federal immigration authorities to protect illegal aliens, even though they are illegal under federal law.

Consequences of Sanctuary Policies

In 2008, San Francisco began a campaign to encourage illegal aliens to take advantage of the city's public services. Mayor Gavin Newsom stated, "We have worked with the Board of

By permission of Michael Ramirez and Creators Syndicate, Inc.

Supervisors, Department of Public Health, labor and immigrant rights groups to create a city government-wide public awareness campaign so that immigrants know the city won't target them for using city services."

The results were tragic. A few months after the campaign, Edwin Ramos, an illegal alien and member of the MS-13 gang, murdered San Francisco resident Tony Bologna and his two sons whom he mistook for rival gang members. Ramos had a lengthy criminal record including a felony assault on a pregnant woman. He was arrested on gang and weapons charges and promptly released just three months before the murder. Not once did San Francisco report him to immigration authorities.

One month after the murder of Bologna, illegal alien Alexander Izaguirre stole Amanda Keifer's purse and then intentionally ran her over with an SUV, laughing as she hit the pavement and fractured her skull. Four months earlier, Alexander Izaguirre had been arrested for felony dealing of crack cocaine. Not only did San Francisco refuse to turn him over to immigration authorities, they expunged his record and helped get him a job, which is criminal in and of itself.

Keifer asked the obvious question, "If they've committed crimes and they're not citizens, then why are they here? Why haven't they been deported?"

The answer is that politicians like Gavin Newsom and Phoenix Mayor [Phil] Gordon put the interests of illegal aliens before the safety of American citizens.

Flaws in Immigration Reform

Our law is already working. One can just scan the newspapers and see dozens of headlines like "Illegal Immigrants Leaving Arizona Over New Law: Tough, Controversial New Legislation Scares Many in Underground Workforce Out of State."

In contrast, American citizens are leaving California. For the last four years, more Americans have left the state than have moved in.

In criticizing the SB 1070, [President] Barack Obama said, "Our failure to act responsibly at the federal level will only open the door to irresponsibility by others." There is nothing irresponsible about enforcing our law, but President Obama is right in that this is only necessary because the federal government does not do its job.

But the solution is not "comprehensive-immigration reform," a euphemism for amnesty.[1] This will only encourage more illegal immigration. And making illegal aliens legal does nothing to change the social and fiscal costs they impose on Arizona or the nation as a whole. The [conservative think tank] Heritage Foundation's research puts the cost of amnesty at over $2.5 trillion dollars.

The federal government simply needs to enforce its immigration laws by cracking down on employers of illegal aliens, securing our borders, and deporting illegal-alien criminals.

1. In the context of illegal immigration, amnesty refers to a governmental pardon for those who have violated federal immigration laws.

This legislation in Arizona will be a model for states across the nation and the federal government, it will end illegal immigration to America, but President Obama is looking towards San Francisco instead.

❙ *"[SB 1070] violates the Constitution."*

Arizona's SB 1070 Immigration Law Is Unconstitutional

Matthew Rothschild

After the signing of Arizona SB 1070, which gave local law enforcement the power to ask any suspect for proof of citizenship, outrage around the country grew as opponents of the legislation decried it as racist and called for a boycott of the state of Arizona. Angered by the bill's passage, Matthew Rothschild takes up the call for a boycott in the following viewpoint, arguing that the bill violates the Constitution. Rothschild contends that many people will be subjected to criminal charges in accordance with SB 1070, harassment of poor Latinos will become the law, and local law enforcement will be granted powers overreaching the boundaries of current law. Rothschild urges all Americans to stand up against these trespasses and support Latino immigrants by boycotting Arizona. Matthew Rothschild is the editor of the Progressive *magazine.*

As you read, consider the following questions:

1. As stated by Rothschild, what does SB 1070 empower local law enforcement to do?

Matthew Rothschild, "Boycott Arizona," *Progressive*, June 2010. Reprinted by permission.

2. What are some of the acts noted by the author that are criminalized by the Arizona law?

3. Why does Rothschild prefer a boycott of Arizona as opposed to allowing the courts to sort out the legality of SB 1070?

The cowardly decision by Arizona Governor Jan Brewer to sign the racist anti-immigrant bill [SB 1070] on April 23 [2010] cannot be allowed to stand. This isn't America when police can stop you and demand your papers because they have a "suspicion" that you may not be here legally.

The Fourth Amendment prevents this kind of police state behavior. It states that people have a right to be "secure in their persons," and that the state must have a warrant and probable cause to search someone.

But the Constitution doesn't seem to apply in Arizona.

Ignoring the Constitution in Arizona

This law empowers local law enforcement to share information about a person who is suspected of being in the U.S. illegally with all levels of government, far and wide. It empowers local law enforcement officers to transport the suspect outside of their jurisdiction. And it lets any local citizen sue the police or local government agencies if that citizen perceives that they are not enforcing federal immigration laws to the fullest extent.

The law also criminalizes almost any kind of aid to someone without proper documentation if the person providing the aid is "in violation of a criminal offense." This may include efforts to transport an undocumented immigrant "if the person knows or recklessly disregards the fact that the alien has come to, has entered, or remains in the United States in violation of law." Providing sanctuary is also verboten [forbidden]: It is forbidden to "attempt to conceal, harbor, or shield an alien from detection in any place in this state, including

121

The Rights of Illegal Immigrants

The rights of unauthorized migrants have evolved in certain patterns that reflect various aspects of a pervasive national ambivalence about immigration outside the law. Because the presence of these noncitizens in the United States is literally outside the law, it would be dissonant—and arguably inconsistent with some ideas that underlie the rule of law—to allow unauthorized migrants to assert legal claims as if their presence were lawful. Yet these migrants live as part of U.S. society in ways that are not just economically and socially important, but also deeply rooted in American history, especially in the complex relationship between the United States and Latin America. To allow their status as unlawful residents to relegate these migrants to legal oblivion would offend other, more fundamental ideas that underlie the rule of law.

Hiroshi Motomura, Duke Law Journal, *May 2010.*

any building or any means of transportation, if the person knows or recklessly disregards the fact that the alien has come to, has entered, or remains in the United States in violation of law."

The new law goes out of its way to enshrine harassment of poor Latinos in Arizona. It makes it illegal to attempt to hire or pick up day laborers if the driver is impeding the normal flow of traffic, or if the worker getting into the car is impeding traffic.

Outrage Spreads

This outrageous law has fortunately sparked a firestorm of condemnation.

Sheriff Clarence Dupnik of Pima County, Arizona, denounced it as "disgusting," "unwise," "stupid," and "racist."

"Governor Brewer and the Arizona legislature have set Arizona apart in their willingness to sacrifice our liberties and the economy of this state," says Alessandra Soler Meetze, executive director of the ACLU [American Civil Liberties Union] of Arizona. "By signing this bill into law, Brewer has just authorized violating the rights of millions of people living and working here. She has just given every police agency in Arizona a mandate to harass anyone who looks or sounds foreign, while doing nothing to address the real problems we're facing."

The religious community has also been outspoken. Jim Wallis, president of Sojourners [a Christian community], says, "This law would force us to violate our Christian conscience, which we simply will not do. It makes it illegal to love your neighbor in Arizona."

Cardinal Roger Mahony of Los Angeles calls it "the country's most retrogressive, mean-spirited, and useless" immigration measure in the land.

John McCullough of the National Council of Churches deems it "reactionary and hateful."

Democrats, including President [Barack] Obama, harshly criticized the law. And even some Republicans did, such as [former Florida governor] Jeb Bush and [senior advisor and deputy chief of staff to President George W. Bush] Karl Rove, who had made an effort at winning over Latinos to the Republican side.

Investigative reporter Greg Palast believes that Brewer actually signed the law to suppress Latino turnout in upcoming elections.

"What moved GOP [Grand Old Party, the Republican Party] Governor Jan Brewer to sign the Soviet-style show-me-your-papers law is the exploding number of legal Hispanics, U.S. citizens all, who are daring to vote—and daring to vote

Democratic by more than two-to-one," says Palast, who notes that Brewer, as secretary of state, tried to disenfranchise voters. "Unless this demographic locomotive is halted, Arizona Republicans know their party will soon be electoral toast."

Brewer, a rightwinger to start with, is facing a tough primary challenge for reelection. She may not have wanted to enrage the rightwing base. But whatever her motives, this heinous law is now on the books.

Americans Should Boycott Arizona

It's time to turn up the heat on Arizona, just as we did when that state was an embarrassing holdout over the Martin Luther King holiday.[1]

More than words are required. Protests, lawsuits, and boycotts are needed.

And they are happening.

The protests began in Arizona even before the governor signed off on the law, and they have continued ever since. On May 1, [2010,] hundreds of thousands of people in cities around the country rallied for immigration rights, with a focus on Arizona.

The lawsuits have also started.

Tucson police officer Martin Escobar filed one of the first suits, saying that the law violates the Constitution and interferes with police work.

The National Coalition of Latino Clergy and Christian Leaders also went to court to seek an injunction on the basis that it violates people's due process rights.

The ACLU and other groups also are considering court challenges, as is the Obama Justice Department.

But putting all of our hopes on the courts would be a mistake. Lawsuits can take a long time. And we can't sit around and wait for the Supreme Court to rule on its obvious uncon-

---

1. Though Martin Luther King Day was named a federal holiday in 1983, Arizona did not acknowledge the holiday until 1992, after a tourist boycott.

stitutionality—especially this current Court. Who knows how the conservative majority would rule?

Better to take nonviolent action and press our case with a boycott.

San Francisco is leading the way. Mayor Gavin Newsom issued an executive order that prevents city officials from traveling on official business to Arizona.

The American Immigration Lawyers Association understandably yanked their fall conference out of Arizona.

And you, as a consumer, should boycott, too. . . .

Scapegoating of Latinos Must Stop

The Arizona law is just the latest manifestation of the ugliness that is marring America right now. Virulent anti-immigrant rhetoric can be heard at almost any tea party [conservative political groups] rally, and it is a feature of many a Republican candidacy. We've seen before in history what happens when a society starts to scapegoat a minority and then codifies this prejudice with laws aimed to humiliate that minority.

The scapegoating of Latino immigrants has got to stop.

And the place to stop it is in Arizona.

And the time to stop it is now.

Periodical and Internet Sources Bibliography

The following articles have been selected to supplement the diverse views presented in this chapter.

Aura Bogado	"Hazing Arizona," *Mother Jones*, July/August 2010.
Susy Buchanan and David Holthouse	"Locked and Loaded," *Nation*, August 28, 2006.
Rachel Ida Buff	"The Deportation Terror," *American Quarterly*, September 2008.
Arian Campo-Flores	"Don't Fence Them In," *Newsweek*, June 7, 2010.
James R. Edwards Jr.	"Arizona Cracks Down on Illegal Immigration," *Human Events*, May 3, 2010.
Daniel Gross et al.	"The New Dream Isn't American," *Newsweek*, May 26, 2008.
Dan Koeppel	"Mending Fences," *Popular Mechanics*, August 2010.
Ginger Thompson	"Work Under Way on 'Virtual Fence,'" *New York Times*, May 9, 2009.
Nathan Thornburgh	"The Battle for Arizona," *Time*, June 14, 2010.

CHAPTER 3

Should US Immigration Policy Be Reformed?

Chapter Preface

Early in 2010, US senators Harry Reid (D-NV), Charles Schumer (D-NY), and Robert Menendez (D-NJ) shaped legislation for comprehensive immigration reform. In part, their proposal—subsequently spearheaded by Schumer and Republican senator Lindsey Graham of South Carolina—would establish a general amnesty for illegal immigrants living in the United States if they admit their illegal status, submit to fingerprinting and background checks, and pay civil fines or perform community service as penance for their criminal entry into the country. The new plan retreads much of the same ground previous amnesty bills have covered—two of which failed to make it out of Congress during the George W. Bush administration. President Barack Obama has thrown his support behind the proposed legislation, hoping that his promise of comprehensive immigration reform will materialize. Opponents in Congress, however, believe this legislation is doomed. Representative Lamar Smith of Texas was quoted by the *Washington Times* on March 18, 2010, as stating, "The bill doesn't have a prayer, because the American people oppose rewarding lawbreakers, which then encourages illegal immigration. . . . Illegal immigrants should return home and play by the rules like millions of legal immigrants."

Although two presidents, Bill Clinton and Ronald Reagan, granted amnesty to illegal aliens in the past, critics charge that these measures actually increased illegal immigration numbers. The US Immigration and Naturalization Service reported that, following the Reagan amnesty in 1986, illegal immigration spiked because relatives of the newly legalized immigrants came to the country to join their families. Writing in *Forbes* on June 10, 2010, coauthor of *The Immigration Solution* Heather Mac Donald, reiterates that conclusion: "An amnesty signals to potential border-crossers that if they can just get into the country illegally, they will eventually be given legal status." Mac Donald goes on to argue that the number of low-skilled workers coming in from Mexico and Latin America is breeding populations of immigrants that are poorly educated, poorly trained, and begetting "second- and third-generation Latinos [who] are assimilating downward into underclass culture." Mac Donald worries that this means more high school dropouts, teen pregnancies, and other social costs that the country must bear. "We must close off the flow of unskilled illegal aliens by enforcing the law, not subverting it with an amnesty," she asserts.

Supporters of the proposed amnesty program state that legalizing citizenship for undocumented workers would likely increase wages because it would halt the exploitation of illegal aliens who often labor in under-the-radar jobs for very little money—an economic factor that drags down wages for all low-skill, low-pay workers. Writing for the Center for American Progress in its 2010 report *Raising the Floor for American Workers: The Economic Benefits of Comprehensive Immigration Reform*, Raúl Hinojosa-Ojeda claims that amnesty would "raise the 'wage floor' for the entire U.S. economy." Using data acquired after the passage of the 1986 Immigration Reform and Control Act (i.e., the Reagan-era amnesty), Hinojosa-Ojeda maintains that evidence indicates comprehensive reform would also "increase consumption, create jobs, and generate additional tax revenue."

As of October 2010, the question of amnesty had not come before the 111th Congress. Other issues have occupied the legislature, and no time frame has been set by the sponsors to advance the proposal. In the following chapter, Raúl Hinojosa-Ojeda presents his argument for amnesty while his peers debate the merits and shortcomings of other immigration policies in the United States.

> "Legalization greatly increases the in-
> centives for formerly unauthorized
> workers to invest in themselves and
> their communities—to the benefit of
> the U.S. economy as a whole."

Illegal Immigrants Should Be Granted Legal Status

Raúl Hinojosa-Ojeda

*Raúl Hinojosa-Ojeda is founding director of the North American
Integration and Development Center at the University of California, Los Angeles. In the following viewpoint, Hinojosa-Ojeda
praises the 1987 Immigration Reform and Control Act for granting legalized status to many undocumented Hispanic immigrants
who had resided continuously in the United States since 1982.
According to the author, these immigrants—freed from the need
to hide from authorities—could vie for better-paying jobs, build
businesses, and contribute to their communities. In Hinojosa-
Ojeda's view, this benefited these workers, raised the wage floor
of all workers, and added wealth to the overall economy. However, Hinojosa-Ojeda notes that the reform measure did not set
flexible quotas to deal with the increasing number of immigrants*

Raúl Hinojosa-Ojeda, *Raising the Floor for American Workers: The Economic Benefits of
Comprehensive Immigration Reform*. Washington, DC: Center for American Progress,
January 2010. Reprinted by permission.

wanting to work in the United States, so within a few years, the pool of illegal immigrants grew again, sinking wages for many legalized immigrants and exacerbating discrimination against Latinos.

As you read, consider the following questions:

1. According to the Westat findings cited by the author, by what percentage did wages for immigrants legalized under the IRCA grow between 1987/1988 and 1992?

2. Besides increased wages, Hinojosa-Ojeda claims that the IRCA gave legalized immigrants powerful incentives to do what two other things?

3. What employer sanctions did the IRCA create to curb the hiring of illegal immigrants who were not given amnesty under the law, according to the author?

The recent history of U.S. immigration policy offers important insights into the economic benefits of providing unauthorized immigrants with legal status and the drawbacks of immigration reform efforts that are not sufficiently comprehensive in scope.

The 1986 IRCA [Immigration Reform and Control Act] granted legal status to 1.7 million unauthorized immigrants through its "general" legalization program, plus another 1.3 million through a "Special Agricultural Workers" program. Even though IRCA was implemented during an economic recession characterized by high unemployment, studies of immigrants who benefited from the general legalization program indicate that they soon earned higher wages and moved on to better jobs—and invested more in their own education so that they could earn even higher wages and get even better jobs.

Higher wages translate into more tax revenue and increased consumer purchasing power, which benefits the public treasury and the U.S. economy as a whole. IRCA failed, how-

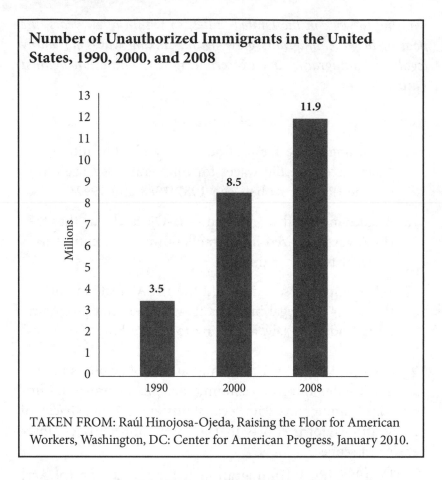

Number of Unauthorized Immigrants in the United States, 1990, 2000, and 2008

TAKEN FROM: Raúl Hinojosa-Ojeda, Raising the Floor for American Workers, Washington, DC: Center for American Progress, January 2010.

ever to create flexible limits on future immigration that were adequate to meet the growing labor needs of the U.S. economy during the 1990s. As a result, unauthorized immigration eventually resumed in the years after IRCA, thereby exerting downward pressure on wages for all workers in low-wage occupations.

Legalized Workers Fare Better

Surveys conducted by [research organization] Westat, Inc. for the U.S. Department of Labor found that the real hourly wages of immigrants who acquired legal status under IRCA's general legalization program had increased an average of 15.1 percent by 1992—four to five years after legalization in 1987 or 1988. Men experienced an average 13.2 percent wage increase and women a 20.5 percent increase during that period. And economists Sherrie Kossoudji and Deborah Cobb-Clark found using the same survey data that 38.8 percent of Mexican men who received legal status under IRCA had moved on to higher-paying occupations by 1992.

Other researchers have also analyzed this survey data and supplemented it with data from additional sources—such as the 1990 Census and the National Longitudinal Survey of Youth—in an effort to determine how much of the wage increase experienced by IRCA beneficiaries was the result of legalization as opposed to the many other variables that influenced wage levels for different workers in different occupations during the same period of time. The findings of these researchers vary according to their economic models, but the results show uniformly positive results for IRCA beneficiaries:

- Economist Francisco Rivera-Batiz estimated that the very fact of having legal status had resulted in a wage increase of 8.4 percent for male IRCA beneficiaries and 13 percent for female IRCA beneficiaries by 1992— independent of any increase in earning power they might have experienced as a result of acquiring more education, improving their mastery of English, or other factors.

- Economists Catalina Amuedo-Dorante, Cynthia Bansak, and Stephen Raphael estimated that real hourly wages had increased 9.3 percent for male IRCA beneficiaries and 2.1 percent for female IRCA beneficiaries by 1992—independent of broader changes in the U.S. economy that might have affected wage levels generally.

- Kossoudji and Cobb-Clark estimated that legalization had raised the wages of male IRCA beneficiaries 6 percent by 1992—independent of broader changes in the U.S. and California economies that might have affected wage levels generally.

Increasing Returns over Time

The experience of IRCA also indicates that legalization greatly increases the incentives for formerly unauthorized workers to invest in themselves and their communities—to the benefit of the U.S. economy as a whole. As Kossoudji and Cobb-Clark explain, the wages of unauthorized workers are generally unrelated to their actual skill level. Unauthorized workers tend to be concentrated in the lowest-wage occupations; they try to minimize the risk of deportation even if this means working for lower wages; and they are especially vulnerable to outright exploitation by unscrupulous employers. Once unauthorized workers are legalized, however, these artificial barriers to upward socioeconomic mobility disappear.

IRCA allowed formerly unauthorized workers with more skills to command higher wages, and also provided a powerful incentive for all newly legalized immigrants to improve their English-language skills and acquire more education so they could earn even more. Kossoudji and Cobb-Clark estimate that if the men who received legal status under IRCA had been "legal" throughout their entire working lives in the United States, their wages by 1992 would have been 24 percent higher because they would have been paid in relation to their actual skill level since arriving in the country and would therefore have had an incentive to improve their skills to further increase their earning power.

A recent North American Integration and Development, or NAID, research project on the 20-year impact of IRCA shows a number of important long-term improvements among previously unauthorized immigrants. The study illustrates that removing the uncertainty of unauthorized status allows legalized immigrants to earn higher wages and move into higher-paying occupations, and also encourages them to invest more in their own education, open bank accounts, buy homes, and start businesses. These are long-term economic benefits that continue to accrue well beyond the initial five-year period examined by most other studies of IRCA beneficiaries.

Reform Must Be Flexible

Unauthorized immigration to the United States initially declined following the passage of IRCA. But IRCA failed to create flexible legal limits on immigration that were capable of responding to ups and downs in future U.S. labor demand. It attempted to stop unauthorized immigration through "employer sanctions" that imposed fines on employers who "knowingly" hire unauthorized workers. Yet it was unable to put an end to unauthorized immigration given the U.S. economy's continuing demand for immigrant labor in excess of existing legal limits on immigration, as well as the ready availability of fraudulent identity documents and the inherent difficulty of proving that an employer has "knowingly" hired an unauthorized worker.

A new, easily exploited unauthorized population arose in the United States during the economic boom of the 1990s. And the costs of employer sanctions were passed along to all Latino workers in the form of lower wages—regardless of legal status or place of birth. This resulted from increased anti-Latino discrimination against job applicants who "looked" like they might be unauthorized, and from the increased use of labor contractors by employers who wanted to distance themselves from the risk of sanctions by having someone else hire workers for them—for a price which was ultimately paid by the workers.

> *"Amnesties do not close floodgates, they open them."*

Illegal Immigrants Should Not Be Granted Legal Status

Paul Belien

In the viewpoint that follows, Paul Belien, the editor of the Brussels Journal, a Belgian news source, argues that the United States can learn a lot from Europe about the dangers of granting amnesty to illegal immigrants. Belien recounts how in the 2000s, various European countries granted legal status to illegal aliens that had lived within their borders for several years. Though these countries, which included Spain, Italy, France, Belgium, and the Netherlands, expected the numbers of applicants for amnesty would be manageable, each nation discovered that hundreds of thousands more immigrants than anticipated showed up for certification. Granting so many amnesties allowed newly legalized immigrants free movement around the European Union and the right to settle in any European nation—even those that kept tight immigration restrictions. In addition, Belien notes that the problem of illegal immigration did not cease after the amnesties. He warns the United States that granting legal status to

Paul Belien, "Let's Not Go Dutch: Amnesty's Track Record in Europe Should Discourage American Imitators," *American Conservative*, vol. 6, no. 16, August 27, 2007, pp. 22–23. Reprinted by permission.

immigrants through general amnesty simply invites more immigrants and exacerbates immigration-related problems.

As you read, consider the following questions:

1. According to Belien, how many illegal immigrants did Italy expect to show up for residency permits when the government granted amnesty in 1998?

2. Why did the expulsion of Ayaan Hirsi Ali cause a liberal backlash in the Netherlands, as the author reports?

3. As Belien explains, why do illegal immigrants who entered the Netherlands after 2001 not fear expulsion after the government granted an amnesty for those who have lived in the country since before 2001?

America is not the only nation debating amnesty for illegal aliens. The issue is a hot topic across the Atlantic as well. On June 8, [2007,] the Dutch Parliament approved a proposal submitted by Nebahat Albayrak, a Turkish-born member of the Dutch government, to give permanent resident cards to everyone who has been living in the Netherlands since 2001. Albayrak, the junior minister of justice, who holds dual Dutch-Turkish citizenship, thinks that some 30,000 will benefit from her amnesty, though no one actually knows how many illegal immigrants are in the country.

If previous amnesties in other Western European countries are any indication, the Dutch may be in for a surprise. Two years ago [in 2005], when Spain announced a collective amnesty for illegal immigrants, the government in Madrid expected that the measure would apply to 300,000 people at most; 800,000 showed up.

Belgium had a similar experience in January 2000, when it granted papers to everyone who had been living in the country illegally for the previous six years. Brussels thought there were 20,000 illegal aliens, but 50,000 applied for amnesty, providing documents, such as doctor's prescriptions, to prove that they had been living in Belgium in 1994. In 1998, when the Italian government announced an amnesty for what was expected to be "fewer than 38,000" illegal immigrants, it had to hand out residence permits to a staggering 220,000.

A History of Amnesties

Amnesties for illegal immigrants take place at regular intervals in Europe. Each time a government grants one, they invariably say that this will be the last and that from now on all illegal newcomers will be expelled. Of course that never happens.

Since 1974, Western Europe has given permanent resident cards to over 5 million illegal immigrants. France has granted three major amnesties in the past 25 years. Spain has offered six in the past 15 years. Italy voted amnesties in 1988, 1990, 1996, 1998, and 2002. Last year, it agreed on another one that allowed over 500,000 people to stay—a figure the government now wants to expand to 1 million. All these countries belong to the European Union [EU], where there is free movement of persons. An amnesty in one country allows the formerly illegal immigrant to move to other EU member states as well.

The largest collective amnesties have been given in Spain, Italy, and Greece. These EU member states, directly bordering Africa and Asia along the Mediterranean, hope that once an illegal alien has obtained his residence permit he will leave for more affluent welfare states like Germany, Britain, or Scandinavia. The immigrants can legally emigrate to a Shangri-La elsewhere in Europe. And, indeed, most of them do.

The Netherlands' Conservative Turn

In the Netherlands, however, the situation is different. The tulip kingdom by the North Sea is as close to paradise as a welfare seeker can get. Those who obtain permission to stay in Holland do not move on, as they have already tapped one of the richest welfare bonanzas on the continent. Hence the puzzling question: why have the Dutch, who had relatively strict immigration policies until the present government took over last February [2007], suddenly decided to open the floodgates? One of the reasons is the role played by someone granted an American green card last year.

Dutch politics resemble a pendulum. From very liberal until the turn of the century, they swung dramatically to the right in the wake of the murders of Pim Fortuyn, a homosexual politician who favored immigration restriction, and Theo van Gogh, an anarchist moviemaker, in 2002 and 2004, respectively. In the resulting shock, the Dutch had to face the fact that many of their newly arrived neighbors were unwilling to accept Holland's traditional liberal tolerance.

Consequently, the strict policies of Rita Verdonk, the minister for integration and immigration in the previous center-right government, initially drew almost unanimous support. "*Nederland is vol*" (The Netherlands are full), the Dutch said. "Iron Rita," a former prison director and head of the state security services, aimed to discourage any non-European fortune seeker from entering, and for a while, the Netherlands had the most uncompromising immigration policies in Europe. Verdonk, a member of the center-right Dutch Liberal Party VVD, even expelled alleged asylum seekers who had already acquired permanent resident cards and sometimes even Dutch citizenship. She took their cards and their citizenship away if they had lied about their real identities or true reasons for entering the country. According to Verdonk, there was no place in Dutch society for people who cheated their way in.

The Ayaan Hirsi Ali Affair

Though Verdonk was reviled by political opponents as a far-right populist, she retained her party's support until May of last year [2006] when it was discovered that Ayaan Hirsi Ali, the most famous Dutch politician at home and abroad and a member of Verdonk's own VVD, was one of the cheaters who had lied their way into the Netherlands and Dutch citizenship.

Ali had come to the Netherlands in 1992 and had obtained political asylum because she claimed to have arrived directly from war-torn Somalia. In reality, although born in Somalia to a prominent, wealthy family, she had been living in Kenya and Germany for the previous 12 years. To disguise her real identity, she used a false name, calling herself Ali instead of Magan, her real name. She also gave the Dutch authorities a false date of birth.

While in the Netherlands, Magan, from then on known as Ali, studied politics. A few years later, she became a Dutch citizen. She gained a reputation as an outspoken critic of Islam and of religion in general and as an activist for women's rights, including abortion. In 2003, she was elected a member of the Dutch Parliament. One year later, she became a global icon of resistance to Islamism when van Gogh was murdered by a Muslim fanatic who left death threats for her on his body. Van Gogh and Hirsi Ali had just finished making a movie entitled "Submission," about discrimination against women in Muslim societies. They were planning a second movie, "Submission 2," about the "Muslim intolerance towards homosexuals."

For the liberal Dutch, and indeed for many elsewhere in the West, including *Reader's Digest*, which elected her "European of the Year," Ali became the Jeanne d'Arc [Joan of Arc] of liberal secularism against Islamism. But when, in May of last year, Dutch television revealed that Magan aka Ali had given false information to enter the Netherlands, Minister Verdonk declared that the immigration rules applied to her as much as to others. Since Ali had committed "identity fraud," she had not legitimately acquired Dutch citizenship, Verdonk argued. She moved to annul her citizenship, whereupon Ali resigned from Parliament. The pro-immigration but anti-

Muslim politician announced that she was leaving for the United States to become a fellow at the American Enterprise Institute.

Liberal Backlash

In the Netherlands, the sudden departure of the "European of the Year" brought a political backlash against Verdonk, who was blamed for chasing the "most famous and courageous Dutch citizen" away. When Iron Rita refused to resign, the government collapsed. The next general elections were won by the Left, which promised an amnesty for illegal aliens as well as for those who had been turned down by Verdonk.

The new Dutch government, a coalition of the Christian-Democrat Party and the Labor Party, is the first government in the Netherlands with immigrant ministers. In addition to Nebahat Albayrak, there is also Ahmed Aboutaleb, secretary of social affairs and employment, who holds dual Moroccan-Dutch citizenship. Both politicians belong to Labor, a party that caters [to] the immigrant vote.

Rita Verdonk, now marginalized even within her own party, has warned that Albayrak's anmesty might attract up to half a million asylum seekers. But the government is not inclined to listen. Verdonk's previous post has gone to Ella Vogelaar, another Labor member, who says that the Netherlands, so far a country of Judeo-Christian traditions, is gradually becoming a "Judeo-Christiano-Islamic" society, a process she considers beneficial. Wouter Bos, the Labor Party leader, who is the current Dutch minister of finance, recently said that he wants to turn the Netherlands into an international center of Sharia [Islamic law] banking, next to Dubai and London.

Never the Last Amnesty

Minister Albayrak told Parliament that the amnesty for everyone who has been living in the Netherlands since 2001 implies that illegal aliens who entered after 2001 have to be expelled.

But she knows that this is not going to happen because the government needs the collaboration of the local authorities to track down illegal aliens. Many mayors, especially those belonging to Albayrak's own Labor Party, have already announced that they will refuse to assist the government in their search for the immigrants.

Amsterdam, Rotterdam, Utrecht, The Hague, and Eindhoven—the five largest cities in the country—refuse to "organize manhunts of illegal immigrants." Ernst Bakker, the mayor of Hilversum, the town where Fortuyn was murdered, told the Dutch press that providing the list of illegal aliens to the government amounts to "betrayal, informing." It reminds him of "Nazi methods."

Some Americans might be inclined to think that an amnesty for illegal immigrants who have already been living in the country for many years might be a good idea, on the condition that it be the final one. But the European experience teaches us that governments always underestimate the number of people who can apply for an amnesty, and that amnesties do not close floodgates, they open them.

> "E-Verify can catch, and is very effective
> at discovering, illegal immigrants."

E-Verify Effectively Deters Illegal Immigration

Jena Baker McNeill

In the viewpoint that follows—a testimony before Congress, Jena Baker McNeill claims that the government should continue to use and expand the Internet worker verification program known as E-Verify. In McNeill's opinion, this service, started by the government in 1997 (and expanded and renamed E-Verify in 2007), is an excellent way for employers to weed out undocumented employees from potential hires because it matches workers' Employment Eligibility Verification form I-9 against government records to see whether the applicants or employees are legally permitted to work in the United States. McNeill encourages the congressional committee to maintain this system because it is an accurate and cost-effective method of deterrence. Jena Baker McNeill is a policy analyst for homeland security at The Heritage Foundation, a conservative public policy research institute in Washington, D.C.

Jena Baker McNeill, "E-Verify: Challenges and Opportunities," Testimony Before Committee on Oversight and Government Reform, Subcommittee on Government Management, Organization, and Procurement, United States House of Representatives, July 23, 2009. Courtesy of Committee on Oversight and Government Reform.

As you read, consider the following questions:

1. In what year was the Immigration Reform and Control Act signed, as reported by McNeill?

2. As the author explains, what two agencies receive the employer-entered E-Verify information?

3. According to McNeill, about what percentage of E-Verify submissions between 2005 and 2007 resulted in a final nonconfirmation status?

An effective immigration policy will be one that has the effect of reducing illegal immigration in the United States. At the same time, policies must center on three goals (1) keeping America free, (2) keeping it safe, and (3) keeping it prosperous. We should not compromise one to gain another; all three can and should be met with respect to America's immigration policies.

E-Verify is a tool that meets these requirements. It tackles the immigration problem by going to the heart of what draws illegal immigrants into the U.S.—finding employment. Illegal immigrants come to America more often than not to find jobs. Proof of this can be seen in the decreased numbers of illegal workers in the United States since the economic downturn. The numbers of individuals crossing the border illegally has dropped significantly since jobs have become scarcer and the recession has deepened. It then follows that if access to employment were curtailed in accordance with the law, many of the current illegal immigrants would leave the country voluntarily and the number of future illegal entrants would be greatly reduced. E-Verify helps to do this in a way that is humane and fair, cost-effective for businesses and the American taxpayer, and maintains privacy. . . .

A History of Lax Enforcement

In 1986, President Ronald Reagan signed the Immigration Reform and Control Act. In exchange for an amnesty of the approximately 3 million illegal workers living in the U.S., Congress promised voters that the government would take effective measures to eliminate future illegal immigration. A major element of this promised policy was increased employment security: measures designed to prevent or reduce significantly the future hiring of illegal immigrants within the U.S.

Until four years ago [2005], however, it was an open secret that once inside the United States; illegal immigrants could live their lives with little fear of arrest or deportation. Essentially, the promise of real enforcement was never fulfilled because illegal workers were able to obtain forged documents purporting to show that they were either lawful immigrants or U.S. citizens. Furthermore, employers were unwilling or unable to verify the authenticity of these documents, making the federal probation on the hiring of illegal workers nearly meaningless.

How E-Verify Works

In 2007, the [George W.] Bush Administration launched an effort to enhance internal enforcement of immigration laws. This effort led to a decline in the number of illegal immigrants inside of the United States. One major component of this strategy was the use of E-Verify (formerly the Basic Pilot/ Employment Eligibility Verification Program).

E-Verify is a system that helps employers to confirm that their newly hired employees are eligible to work in the United States by verifying their information on a Web-based system run by the Department of Homeland Security (DHS) and the Social Security Administration (SSA). The following basic steps occur:

1. An employer enters the employee's information into an online portal; such as the employee's name, date of birth, and Social Security number.

145

2. The information is securely transmitted to DHS and SSA. DHS checks the information against both DHS and SSA databases to determine whether it corresponds to a U.S. citizen or work-eligible immigrant. In most cases, DHS can do this and transmit a definitive reply to the employer within seconds.

3. If the information cannot be corroborated by the USCIS [US Citizenship and Immigration Services] automated check, the case is referred to a USCIS immigration status verifier, who checks the employee's information against other DHS databases.

4. If the employee information is corroborated by the SSA database, the USCIS automated database, or by the immigration status verifier's review, DHS sends the employer an electronic positive confirmation notice certifying that the employee is an eligible worker. Ninety-four percent of E-Verify submissions receive initial positive confirmations, most within three to five seconds.

5. If the information submitted by the employee does not match any information in the SSA and USCIS records, E-Verify automatically gives the employer the opportunity to double check the submitted information for clerical errors. If clerical errors are found, the employee's data can be resubmitted immediately, and a positive confirmation can be received from DHS within seconds. If no clerical errors are found, or if the information still does not match any information in SSA or USCIS records, then E-Verify issues a *tentative non-confirmation* to the employee.

6. In the case of a *tentative non-confirmation*, the employee has eight federal working days to correct the non-confirmation at a local SSA office (if he/she is a citizen) or a USCIS office (if he/she is a lawful immigrant).

These errors can be resolved quite simply by a toll-free phone call. Ninety-five percent of contested non-confirmations are resolved with a single phone call or appointment.

7. If the employee chooses not to contest the tentative non-confirmation or has not provided information to alter the non-confirmation within eight working days, DHS sends a *final non-confirmation* to the employer electronically.

8. After receipt of a *final non-confirmation*, the employer must either (a) discharge the employee or (b) notify DHS that it plans to continue employment. This allows employers to continue employment in situations where they are certain the non-confirmation is incorrect and will be rectified at some point.

An Effective Enforcement Tool

At present, more than 87,000 employers participate in E-Verify voluntarily. Contributing to this success is that E-Verify helps employers enforce immigration laws in a cheap and user-friendly fashion. For example, the software is free and requires very basic information—information already found on the I-9 [employment eligibility form]. Specifically, the program has the following benefits:

Accuracy and Speed. E-Verify can determine quickly and accurately the authenticity of the personal information and credentials offered by new hires. The accuracy of E-Verify was confirmed in 2007 by a formal evaluation of E-Verify/Basic Pilot for DHS by Westat, an influential private research firm. From October 2005–March 2007, Westat found:

- More than 90 percent of submissions received an initial positive confirmation; around 1 percent of submissions received an initial tentative non-confirmation that was contested and converted into a final positive confirma-

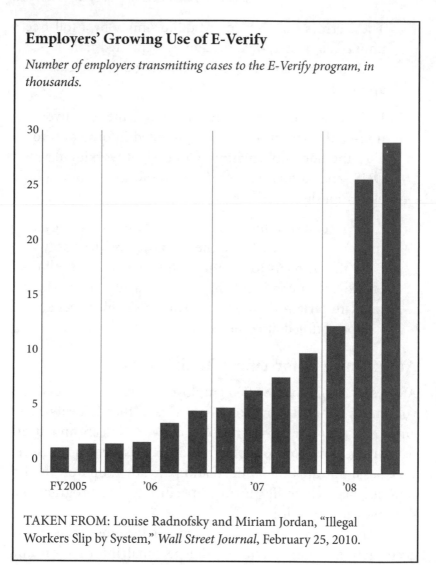

Employers' Growing Use of E-Verify

Number of employers transmitting cases to the E-Verify program, in thousands.

TAKEN FROM: Louise Radnofsky and Miriam Jordan, "Illegal Workers Slip by System," *Wall Street Journal*, February 25, 2010.

tion once information discrepancies were corrected; and around 7 percent of submissions resulted in final non-confirmations, nearly all resulting from initial tentative non-confirmations that were never contested.

- Among all employees who were eventually found to be work-authorized, 99.4 percent received an initial positive confirmation, and 0.6 percent received an initial tentative non-confirmation that was corrected by a brief visit to an SSA or USCIS office.

- The evaluation found around 5 percent of final non-confirmations under the system may have been authorized workers. However, there were no reported instances in which authorized workers who received a tentative non-confirmation were unable to contest the ruling successfully and establish proper work authorization.

Overall, the evaluation showed that E-Verify was very successful in distinguishing between authorized and unauthorized workers. It also provides a process for correcting erroneous initial findings. Despite years of use and screenings of millions of employees, there has never been a single instance in which a lawful worker lost permanent employment as a result of erroneous information provided by the E-Verify system. . . .

Low Cost to Business. E-Verify can be done in a cost-effective manner, so that businesses, regardless of size, can check the legal status of their employees without breaking the bank. Of course, even though the software is free, there is some cost to business from using E-Verify. But the Westat evaluation found low employer costs to set up the system and operate it over a year. For instance, the evaluation found that:

- Firms with between 100 and 250 employees reported average setup costs and annual operating expenses of $646, or around $4.00 per standing employee;

- Firms with 251 to 500 employees reported average costs of $746, or around $2.00 per employee; and

- Firms with between 501 and 1,000 employees reported average setup and annual operating costs of $473, or less than $1.00 per employee.

Furthermore, knowing beforehand that an employee can legally work will minimize the cost of having to hire new employees later. . . .

Maintains Privacy. The only personal information entered into E-Verify is the employee's name, date of birth, Social Security number, and citizenship status. This information is already included in the official I-9 forms that the employer completes for each employee. E-Verify does not allow employers to examine information from the Social Security Administration or other government agencies. Furthermore, the government already has this information in its records and routinely collects similar information as part of the new-hire process and for purposes of collecting income and FICA [Federal Insurance Contributions Act; i.e., Social Security contribution] taxes. The DHS employees who operate the E-Verify system only have access to the information submitted through E-Verify and the SSA confirmation or non-confirmation of that information. They do not have access to the larger SSA employment history and earnings files for individuals nor can DHS employees view or examine SSA records; they can merely corroborate that the limited identity data submitted for an individual through E-Verify matches information in the SSA files.

Room for Improvement

Perhaps the biggest challenge facing E-Verify at this time is the future viability of the program. If Congress does not reauthorize E-Verify by September 30, 2009 it will expire. Furthermore, DHS has yet to implement the federal contractors provision signed by President Bush in June of 2008. This executive order directs all federal departments and agencies to require contractors (as a condition for obtaining future federal contracts) to agree to use E-Verify. This is a needed provision given the recent stimulus, where hundreds of thousands of new construction jobs are coming available—and should go to those lawfully able to work in the U.S., given the near record high unemployment. At present, all federal employees are checked by the E-Verify system, but outside contractors receiving federal funds are not required to use the system.

E-Verify is not without its challenges, however, and it should be the burden of DHS and Congress to work together to continually drive down its already low error rates and find ways to enforce the law in areas E-Verify is not effective. For example, E-Verify cannot catch either identity fraud or "off the books" employment. In an identity fraud situation, the illegal employee presents identity documents to the employer showing that he is either a U.S. citizen or lawful immigrant entitled to work. However, in this case, the name, date of birth, Social Security number and (in some cases) the green card number on the documents corresponds to the identity of a real U.S. citizen or lawful immigrant. E-Verify can catch, and is very effective at discovering, illegal immigrants working under a fictitious Social Security number, green card number, name, and/or date of birth—significantly reducing the opportunity to work illegally. . . .

Keeping an Effective System Working for America

Government policy should be based on the principles of *empowerment, deterrence,* and *information.* It should empower honest employers by giving them the tools to determine quickly and accurately whether a new hire is an authorized worker. It should hold employers free from penalty if they inadvertently hire an illegal worker after following the prescribed procedures.

E-Verify is the most promising employment verification system in existence in the United States, and it should be continued. But the future of E-Verify is in the hands of Congress. It should be permanently reauthorized and fully funded in order to expand and be used effectively.

| *"Big, uniform identity systems do not work well."*

E-Verify Does Not Significantly Deter Illegal Immigration

Jim Harper

Jim Harper is director of information policy studies at the Cato Institute, a libertarian public policy research organization in Washington, D.C. He is also the author of Identity Crisis: How Identification Is Overused and Misunderstood. *In the following viewpoint, Harper claims that E-Verify, the system that checks whether workers have the eligibility to hold jobs in the United States, is flawed. In Harper's view, E-Verify has the potential to deny work to eligible workers due to data entry mistakes or other errors. He maintains that the system may have some effect on controlling illegal immigration, but he believes most immigrants will find ways to take advantage of the identity theft problem in the United States to get correct documentation to fool electronic verification or will simply find less-scrupulous employers who will pay "under the table" to avoid the costs of using the system. Most worrisome for Harper, though, is the social costs of using*

Jim Harper, "Electronic Employment Eligibility Verification: Franz Kafka's Solution to Illegal Immigration," Cato Policy Analysis No. 612, March 5, 2008. Reprinted with permission.

such a large-scale surveillance. He argues that it will increase discrimination on the part of employers who will not take the risk of hiring Hispanic workers (the ethnic group that makes up the largest percentage of illegal aliens), and he envisions that such a system will lead to broader government monitoring of all Americans.

As you read, consider the following questions:

1. What legislation inaugurated the pilot program that became E-Verify, as Harper reports?

2. According to the author, what percentage of employers using the pilot program had received a tentative non-confirmation for an employee caused by data entry mistakes?

3. Why does Harper believe law-abiding, legal workers might be unnecessarily punished by the E-Verify system?

The nation's immigration policy is at a crossroads. According to Labor Department projections, the U.S. economy, which is already near full employment [in March 2008], will continue to create 400,000 or more low-skilled jobs annually in the service sector—tasks like food preparation, cleaning, construction, landscaping, and retail sales. Yet from 1996 to 2004, the number of adult Americans without a high school education—the demographic that typically fills those jobs—fell by 4.6 million.

These demographic facts create very powerful economic forces. Demand in the United States for both low- and high-skilled workers is high, and workers in many nearby countries badly need the work offered in the United States. The economic gradient is steep.

Just as water follows the laws of gravity, workers continually move to the United States. Unlike water, however, which simple barriers can stop, people on both sides of the border dedicate their ingenuity to getting what they want and need. The self-interest of employers and workers is a powerful (and almost always beneficial) force that is hard to quell or conquer. Thus, migration into the United States has persisted over the last several decades.

Today, however, the political consensus holds that the country has too many immigrants and that something must be done about it. A part of that consensus is that internal enforcement of immigration law should be strengthened, including by electronic employment eligibility verification [EEV]. EEV requires employers to run background checks with the government on new or existing employees to see whether they are eligible to work under the immigration laws.

A full-fledged EEV system has many practical and technical problems, to say nothing of the question of whether it is appropriate for a free country. But the human forces that a policy would channel or counteract are the most important influences on how the supporting technical system must be designed. Those forces determine where the challenges to the system will come from and what the human and monetary costs will be if it is to work for its intended purpose. Immigration law—today deeply at odds with Americans' interests—is the source of the problem and the starting point for analysis. . . .

By the 1980s, the United States was seeing a strong flow of immigrants from Mexico and Central America. This paralleled earlier flows from Germany, Ireland, Italy, and elsewhere, but these immigrants could enter through uncontrolled parts of a land border without documentation. In 1986 Congress determined that illegal immigration rates were too high, but in passing the Immigration Reform and Control Act [IRCA], Congress failed to recognize rather the power of the economic forces underlying such immigration or its benefits.

While legalizing the illegal aliens in the country, Congress declined to expand legal channels for immigration. Instead, it changed the long-standing natural rule that working in the United States depended simply on willingness and ability. Americans' right to earn an honest living by trading their labor would now have to wait for proof of compliance with federal immigration laws.

Evolution of I-9 Enforcement

IRCA made unlawful the knowing hire of workers who are not eligible to work in the United States under the immigration laws. By requiring employers to check employees' documentation, the law conscripted employers into immigration law enforcement. All employers today are required to verify employees' work eligibility by collecting completed I-9 forms and by checking employees' documentation.

The logic behind this idea was simple: making it illegal to hire an illegal immigrant could reduce the strength of this country's economic "magnet." But the policy of "internal enforcement" built on this simple logic failed. Just as a magnet's attraction passes through paper, the attraction of the United States to immigrants surpasses this paperwork.

The I-9 process and employer sanctions undoubtedly had some effect on illegal immigration and working, but not very much. Between 1986 and 1996, illegal immigration rates appear to have remained steady. Document fraud undermined the I-9 system, and the law prompted some employers to discriminate wrongly against citizens and legal immigrants because of their Hispanic surnames, poor English-language skills, or appearance.

Ten years later, with illegal immigration continuing apace, the Illegal Immigration Reform and Immigrant Responsibility Act of 1996 sought to "improve on" the failing policy of internal enforcement. It required the Immigration and Naturalization Service to commence three pilot programs to test electronic verification of employees' work eligibility. These were the Citizen Attestation Verification Pilot Program, the

Machine-Readable Document Pilot Program, and the Basic Pilot Program. These three programs were intended to test whether verification procedures could make the existing Form I-9 process better by (1) reducing document fraud and false claims of U.S. citizenship, (2) discouraging discrimination against employees, (3) avoiding violations of civil liberties and privacy, and (4) minimizing the burden on employers to verify employees' work eligibility. . . .

Basic Pilot—first renamed the "employment eligibility verification" program, or EEV, and then renamed again, "E-Verify"—is the remaining effort to verify work eligibility electronically. As of May 2007, about 9,000 of the 17,000 employers registered for the system were active users. Currently, about 52,000 of the country's 5.9 million employers have registered for it—about .88 percent. Congress extended the Basic Pilot program in January 2002 and again in December 2003. . . .

How Electronic Employment Verification Works

After collecting I-9 forms, participating employers enter the information supplied by workers into a government website. The system compares these data with information held by the Social Security Administration [SSA] and with DHS [Department of Homeland Security] databases. If the name and SSN [Social Security number] pairs match to citizen data at the SSA, a worker is approved. The system compares information from noncitizens with DHS data to determine whether the employee is eligible to work.

E-Verify electronically notifies employers whether their employees' work authorization is confirmed. Submissions that the automated check cannot confirm are referred to U.S. Citizenship and Immigration Service staff in the Department of Homeland Security, who take further steps to verify eligibility or who find the worker ineligible.

When E-Verify cannot confirm a worker's eligibility, it issues the employer a "tentative nonconfirmation." The employer must notify the affected worker of the finding, and the worker has the right to contest his or her tentative nonconfirmation within eight working days by contacting the SSA or DHS.

When a worker does not contest his or her tentative nonconfirmation within the allotted time, the E-Verify program issues a final nonconfirmation for the worker. The employer is required to either immediately terminate the worker or notify DHS that it continues to employ the worker—confessing to a law violation. . . .

Errors Idle Eligible Workers

A nationwide EEV system would send a substantial number of workers—native-born and legal immigrant alike—into labyrinthine bureaucratic processes, preventing them from working until the federal government deemed their papers to be in order. It would be more like something out of a Franz Kafka novel than a sound U.S. federal policy. EEV would delay or deny the employment of American workers in numerous ways.

Think of electronic employment verification as a screen through which all workers would have to pass before they could earn a living. The problem is to get eligible workers through the screen quickly and to keep ineligible workers from passing through. It is hard to do both at the same time. The federal government currently has only fragments of the infrastructure for accomplishing this goal, and the processes for doing so are rife with flaws.

For example, simple errors in transcription and data entry by employees and employers will create a baseline wrongful tentative nonconfirmation rate. According to a recent survey of employers participating in Basic Pilot, 52 percent had received at least one tentative nonconfirmation for a new employee caused by data entry mistakes.

The Critical Flaw in the System

Industry experts say the I-9 employee-verification process, which requires all potential employees to provide documents that prove identity and employment eligibility in the U.S., is porous and easily manipulated (either by false applicants or shady employers looking to hire illegal workers). The critical flaw of the system, experts say, is that it relies solely on documents the new employee is presenting.

Nick Diulio, QSR Magazine,
October 2009. www.qsrmagazine.com.

Then we must consider the error rate in federal government databases. In December 2006, the SSA's Office of the Inspector General estimated that the agency's "Numident" file—the data against which Basic Pilot checks worker information—has an error rate of 4.1 percent. Every error resulted in Basic Pilot's providing incorrect results. At that rate, 1 in every 25 new hires would receive a tentative nonconfirmation. At 55 million new hires each year, this rate produces about 11,000 tentative nonconfirmations per workday in the United States—a little more than 25 people per congressional district, each day of the working week, all year long. . . .

Counterattacks and Complications

Immigrants and employers dedicate their ingenuity to getting what they want and need. Although a national EEV system would reduce the growth in illegal immigration by some measure, it would also prompt illegal immigrants and some employers to undertake a variety of countermeasures.

For example, more people would work "under the table." Workers and employers would collude—even more often than they do now—to avoid the already substantial regulatory hassles and costs of working on the books. With the increased liability for employers who did comply with the Form I-9 process, following the letter of the law would be riskier, and violating the law by going underground would be relatively more attractive.

Avoidance of EEV would be one result of strengthened internal enforcement. But a variety of counterattacks on the EEV system would be part of the response as well. They would create extraordinary new costs and complexities that would burden U.S. workers while weakening EEV's deterrence to illegal employment and immigration.

One counterattack on the EEV system that illegal immigrants would adopt is a mere shift in strategy. Today, many submit false documentation of plausible names and SSNs for the Form I-9 process. This technique would not pass EEV, of course: the name and SSN must match in the SSA's records.

In response, illegal immigrants would adjust their frauds so that they use name and SSN pairs that match. It is slightly more difficult to do but easily worthwhile to procure "legal" work.

To respond to this attack, the EEV system would monitor the use of name and SSN pairs. When a name and SSN were used too often in succession, or in different parts of the country, the system would "flag" the name and SSN pair. Its users would be suspected of fraud, and they would be tentatively nonconfirmed.

However, this response would have costs. One, of course, is that it requires a federal database that records every new hire in the country—yet another of many incremental increases in the tracking of law-abiding Americans. None of them are terribly objectionable by themselves, but the totality is quite concerning.

A more immediate cost is that law-abiding citizens would regularly stand accused of identity fraud. The SSA and DHS would not know which user of a name-SSN pair was the genuine person and which was using a false identity. EEV would tentatively nonconfirm all users of that name-SSN pair. The "true" individuals attached to fraudulently used identities would learn of identity fraud in their names when they were refused work by EEV and plunged into a bureaucratic morass.

Today, identity fraud creates financial difficulties for innocent victims when they find that their financial reputations have been sullied. EEV would also make them unemployable.

Illegal immigrants would counterattack in response to the tracking of name-SSN pairs by using *original* name-SSN pairs with each new hire. EEV would cause illegal aliens to seek out name-SSN pairs that have not been used recently in employment. It would create a bigger criminal market for American citizens' personal information. . . .

Corrupting the System

Yet another attack on the EEV system would be to corrupt the federal employees who handle tentative nonconfirmations. As so often happens in departments of motor vehicles (DMVs) across the country, criminals would find federal workers willing to use their access—or fellow workers' logins—to "confirm" people operating under false identities. Doing so may well exclude from work the people whose identities are being used.

Consider also how employers would protect themselves. With illegal immigrants today coming predominantly from Spanish-speaking countries south of the U.S. border, identity fraud and corruption attacks on the EEV system would focus largely on Hispanic surnames and given names. Recognizing that Hispanic employees—even native-born citizens—are more often caught up in identity fraud and tentative nonconfirmation hassles, employers would select against Hispanics in their hiring decisions. . . .

Toward National Surveillance

People angered by illegal immigration are undoubtedly frustrated that internal enforcement works so poorly and that our systems provide so little security against people entering the country illegally. This is simply because big, uniform identity systems do not work well. As Phillip J. Windley, the former chief information officer of Utah, observes in his book *Digital Identity*:

> Visions that a centralized approach will promote security, cost savings, or management simplicity are a mirage. Centralized digital identity systems do not scale. Identity relationships are inherently web-like in structure, while centralized technologies like directories are hierarchical.

In other words, identity works well in one-on-one transactions, in groups, and in voluntary organizations. People and businesses naturally collect the identifiers and other information they need for meetings, contracts, dates, employment, friendship, and so on. But people do not have a single identity that can be captured and applied to all their relationships. As Windley points out, relationships define the many different identities people have. Identities do not define relationships—at least not in a modern, free country.

Bringing Americans into a uniform government identity system—for controlling illegal immigration or any other purpose—would make people's relationship with government one of the foremost in their lives. It would be an attempt to force a relationship on them that many do not want. But a successful EEV system—indeed, successful internal enforcement of federal immigration law—requires this kind of overweening, unworkable, and unacceptable identity system.

| "Community policing [or sanctuary]
| policies make all of us safer."

Sanctuary Policies Make Americans Safer

Lynn Tramonte

Lynn Tramonte argues in the following viewpoint that "sanctuary city" policies in American cities help keep communities safe. Sanctuary policies, the author explains, allow illegal immigrants to report crimes and give testimony against criminals without fear of deportation. Tramonte claims these policies are sound because they serve the public good by helping law enforcement catch criminals. Tramonte believes Congress needs to pass comprehensive immigration legislation that effectively deals with immigration problems while not dismantling community programs—such as sanctuary policies—that benefit Americans. Lynn Tramonte is the deputy director of America's Voice, an organization dedicated to humane immigration reform.

As you read, consider the following questions:

1. According to Tramonte, what was the Los Angeles Police Department's Special Order 40?

Lynn Tramonte, "Debunking the Myth of 'Sanctuary Cities': Community Policing Policies Protect American Communities," Immigration Policy Center Special Report, March 2009. Reprinted by permission.

2. As the author reports, how many cities and states in America have adopted policies that prevent police agencies from asking community residents who have not been arrested to prove their legal immigration status?

3. Why does Tramonte question the mission of the Department of Homeland Security–sponsored Fugitive Operation Teams?

In Providence, Rhode Island, Guatemalan immigrant Danny Sigui helped convict a murderer by providing critical testimony against the accused. During preparation of the case, the state attorney general's office learned that Sigui was an undocumented immigrant, and reported him to the U.S. Department of Homeland Security (DHS). Sigui was deported following the trial. When asked whether he would have come forward again, knowing that doing so would lead to his deportation, Sigui replied: "If I had known they would take my liberty, that they would take my children away from me, that they would put me [in immigration detention], I would not do this." Without Sigui's testimony in the case, a murderer might have gone free. With Sigui's testimony, his subsequent deportation, and the publicity around it, one murderer is behind bars, but more criminals are free to prey on victims silenced by his example.

Historically, the federal government has enforced civil immigration law and state and local police have focused on enforcing criminal law. However, propelled by increased frustration with the nation's broken immigration system, renewed focus on immigration enforcement, and anti-immigrant sentiment, demands for state and local police to take on an increased role in immigration enforcement have grown exponentially.

The Public Working with Police

State and local police already have the authority to arrest anyone suspected of criminal activity, including non-citizens, and police regularly work with DHS to identify foreign-born criminals, detain them, and transport them for eventual deportation. However, most police do *not* arrest immigrants solely for being undocumented. To date, most state and local police have rejected calls for "deputization" in immigration law enforcement because they believe it makes it more difficult for them to protect their communities. As Sigui's case illustrates, there is a real cost to this shift that damages local residents' trust in the police and undermines public safety.

More than 50 cities and states across the country have adopted policies that prevent police agencies from asking community residents who have not been arrested to prove their legal immigration status. These policies do allow state and local police to report foreign-born criminals to DHS. Based on the tenets of community policing, these policies make it safe for immigrant crime victims and witnesses to report criminals to the police and help put them behind bars. Critics claim that these cities and states provide "sanctuary" to criminals, but research shows that the opposite is true. Crime experts, including hundreds of local police officers, have found that cities with community policing policies do work closely with DHS and have built bridges to immigrant communities that have improved their ability to fight crime and protect all residents.

Evolution of the Sanctuary Movement

There is much confusion about the term "sanctuary city." The term is often used derisively by immigration opponents to blast what are best described as community policing policies. In fact, these community policing policies are about providing safety, not sanctuary, to the residents of U.S. communities.

The phrase "sanctuary city" is a relic of decades-old policies. In the 1980s, thousands of Central American refugees came to the United States seeking protection from civil wars raging in the region. Initially, many were denied asylum in the

United States due to Cold War politics, and were therefore "undocumented." Churches, synagogues, and other religious institutions banded together to oppose the return of these refugees to the countries where they had been persecuted. These institutions became part of the Sanctuary Movement, a sort of "underground railroad" for Salvadoran and Guatemalan asylum-seekers which helped with legal representation, employment, and other basic needs. Some cities pledged solidarity with the Sanctuary Movement and opposition to the government's treatment of these refugees. Eventually, through lawsuits and changes to federal law, most of the asylum-seekers won a second chance at legal immigration status, and many are now U.S. citizens.

The concept of community policing began taking shape in the late 1970s, however, before the Sanctuary Movement began. Cities with growing immigrant populations began adapting the community policing framework to their changing communities. In 1979, the Los Angeles Police Department issued Special Order 40, which prohibits police officers from inquiring about the immigration status of people not suspected of crimes. According to the policy, which remains in effect today [in March 2009], "participation and involvement of the undocumented alien community in police activities will increase the Department's ability to protect and serve the entire community." In addition to reassuring immigrant crime victims that they can report their attackers without risking deportation, the Los Angeles policy instructs officers on how to refer non-citizens arrested for crimes to federal authorities. As the promise of community policing took root, many other cities with large immigrant populations enacted policies like Los Angeles'.

After 9/11, immigration enforcement actions conducted in the name of fighting terrorism began to chill immigrant contact with state and local police. As a way to re-establish trust with immigrant residents and encourage crime reporting by all, more cities and states enacted community policing policies based on the Los Angeles model. Some of these policies were enacted by legislative bodies, while others were issued as executive orders. Still others exist as police department general orders or operating instructions, and a few were even mandated by the courts due to lawsuits challenging unlawful immigration enforcement actions by police. These community policing policies now exist in towns large and small, from Portland, Maine to Portland, Oregon, and many places in between.

Keeping Communities Safe

State and local police departments around the country support these community policing policies because they encourage immigrants to work with the police to put criminals behind bars. According to San Jose, California Police Chief Rob Davis, "we have been fortunate enough to solve some terrible cases because of the willingness of illegal immigrants to step forward, and if they saw us as part of the immigration services, I just don't know if they'd do that anymore. That would affect our mission, which I thought was to protect and serve our community."

The International Association of Chiefs of Police (IACP), the nation's premier law enforcement association, voiced its perspective in a 2004 policy paper, "Enforcing Immigration Law: The Role of State, Tribal and Local Law Enforcement." According to the IACP, "local police agencies depend on the cooperation of immigrants, legal and illegal, in solving all sorts of crimes and in the maintenance of public order. Without assurances that they will not be subject to an immigration investigation and possible deportation, many immigrants with critical information would not come forward, even when heinous crimes are committed against them or their families." Federal legislation that would sanction police departments unless they reversed their community policing policies was deemed "unacceptable" by this law enforcement institution.

In 2006, the Major Cities Chiefs Association (MCCA), a group of police chiefs from the sixty-four largest police departments in the United States and Canada, issued a similar policy statement. According to the MCCA, "without assurances that contact with the police would not result in purely civil immigration enforcement action, the hard won trust, communication and cooperation from the immigrant community would disappear. Such a divide between the local police and immigrant groups would result in increased crime against immigrants and in the broader community, create a class of silent victims and eliminate the potential for assistance from immigrants in solving crimes or preventing future terroristic acts."

These law enforcement experts understand that the entire community suffers when a portion of the population is too fearful to cooperate with the police. Many immigrant families are "mixed status" families, comprised of U.S. citizens, legal permanent residents, and undocumented immigrants. The fear of deportation among immigrant families is so intense that even legal residents and U.S. citizens can be afraid to contact law enforcement unless they know it is "safe" to do so.

Building Trust

Criminal justice expert David A. Harris, a professor at the University of Pittsburgh School of Law, writes that immigrants are often preyed upon by criminals who assume they will be less likely to contact the police out of fear of deportation. In his book *Good Cops: The Case for Preventive Policing*, Harris says police can help combat that vulnerability and put more criminals behind bars by keeping the immigration status of crime victims and witnesses confidential, and communicating this policy clearly to the immigrant community. According to Harris, after a wave of violent robberies in Austin, Texas,

Assistant Police Chief Rudy Landeros launched an outreach campaign to encourage Latinos of all immigration statuses to report crimes to the police. His police department told the community: "Trust us. We are not Immigration, we are not going to arrest you, and we are not going to deport you." As a result of the Department's efforts, reports of armed robberies grew by 20 percent, and over 150 serial criminals were arrested.

Advocates for crime victims agree that these community policing policies are essential to encouraging immigrants to access police protection. Leslye Orloff, Director of the Immigrant Women Program of Legal Momentum (formerly the NOW Legal Defense and Education Fund), testified before the House Judiciary Subcommittee on Immigration, Border Security, and Claims that "fear of being reported to [immigration authorities] and of subsequent deportation is one of the most significant factors preventing immigrant victims of domestic violence from seeking help from legal and social service systems." In her testimony, Orloff recommended that all cities and states adopt community policing policies that encourage immigrants to report crimes without fear of deportation.

In the report *Balancing Federal and Local Priorities in Police-Immigrant Relations*, Michele Wucker, Executive Director of the World Policy Institute, provides a snapshot of how relations between police and the immigrant community have been managed successfully in Portland, Oregon since 9/11. This city has a resolution affirming a provision in the state code that prevents state and local police from investigating or detaining persons who have not violated criminal laws, even though they may have committed a civil immigration law violation.

According to the report, the city of Portland has cultivated a strong working relationship with members of the Muslim, South Asian, Arab, and immigrant communities over the course of several years through a commitment to two-way dialogue and incorporating the communities' concerns into city business. After 9/11, the Portland Police Department helped establish a community advisory organization made up of Arab and Muslim community leaders; acted promptly to address safety concerns faced by members of the Muslim, Arab, and South Asian communities experiencing hate crimes; and refused to participate in certain federal law enforcement programs that targeted residents based on national origin or religion instead of conduct. According to Wucker, "the Portland police department's refusal to implement the [George W.] Bush administration's calls for enforcing federal policy bolstered local Muslims' sense of security, as did police-community dialogue and the police department's commitment to working with immigrant groups."

Policies That Undermine Trust

Unfortunately, examples of state and local police involvement in the deportation of non-criminals also exist, and send powerful messages to local communities that dismantle community trust. The case of Danny Sigui ... is but one example. During the October 2002 sniper rampage in the Washington, DC area, many immigrants were fearful of approaching the authorities with tips and information. The arrest and deportation of a pair of undocumented workers who were not involved in the crimes, but simply used a phone booth staked out by the investigative team, validated those fears. Following this highly visible development, Montgomery County, Maryland Police Chief Charles Moose had to take to the airwaves and make a plea to the region's immigrant residents, asking for their cooperation. INS [Immigration and Naturalization Service] Commissioner James Ziglar also tried to reassure immigrants that the INS would not question the immigration status of those who came forward with information, but the damage to community trust was done.

More recently, some state and local police efforts to assist DHS in deporting undocumented "criminals" have begun to chill immigrants' relationships with the police. A number of state and local agencies have entered into agreements with the DHS and received training in immigration law under what is known as the "287(g)" program. Some received this training in order to better assist DHS in conducting immigration screenings of convicted criminals. Still others have used the training in order to operate as *de facto* immigration agents, and ask residents they come across in traffic stops or other routine situations to prove they are legally present in the United States. Under this program, many undocumented immigrants have been arrested and deported for minor offenses related to their status as undocumented workers, such as driving without a license. In addition, state and local police have participated in DHS "Fugitive Operations Teams" that often go to the homes of non-criminal, undocumented workers with outstanding deportation orders to arrest them. These initiatives were initially billed as discreet in nature and limited to criminal apprehensions, but the reality has been quite different. A February 2009 study by the Migration Policy Institute [a nonpartisan research organization] found that 73% of the individuals apprehended by Fugitive Operations Teams had no criminal convictions; in 2007, fugitives with criminal convictions represented just 9% of total Fugitive Operations Team arrests. The others arrested are "collaterals" that the teams find in homes, neighborhoods, strip malls, and other locations while they are searching for those identified as violent criminals. Because undocumented immigrants see the police arresting people who are not hardened criminals but rather workers without papers just like them, they are becoming more fearful that cooperating with the police could have the same result for them or their loved ones. . . .

Congress needs to enact a federal immigration law that will restore control and order to our immigration system by screening the existing population of undocumented immigrants; isolating the few bad apples who should not be allowed to remain in the United States because they've committed crimes; requiring the rest to legalize their status; and fixing the problems with our system that created this build-up of undocumented immigrants in the first place. An important piece of this law would be a smart and effective enforcement regime, but the idea that we could deport our way to a solution—or ask state and local police agencies to step in where the federal government has failed—is counterproductive at best.

Until Congress acts to fix this problem comprehensively, state and local governments will be under pressure to deal with the consequences of our broken system. Scores of police departments around the country have decided to make public safety their number-one priority, and reject politicians' demands that would undermine their efforts to fight crime. Their community policing policies make all of us safer. The cities and states that actively encourage police to enforce civil immigration laws are the real "sanctuaries" for criminals, because they are alienating a segment of the community that experiences crime but is afraid to report it.

| "Providing sanctuary for law-breakers at the expense of law-abiding citizens is neither a compassionate nor a moral approach."

Sanctuary Policies Make Americans Less Safe

Cinnamon Stillwell

Cinnamon Stillwell is a writer living in San Francisco. In the following viewpoint, she claims that San Francisco's "sanctuary" policy regarding illegal immigrants makes citizens less safe. Stillwell believes a policy that compels law enforcement to maintain a hands-off stance toward illegal immigrants can have tragic consequences. As she explains, lax policing of immigrants has resulted in brutal crimes in San Francisco, while the detention of illegal aliens has unnecessarily drained city funds. Stillwell contends that the city should turn illegal immigrants over to federal authorities for deportation so that the public can rest easier.

As you read, consider the following questions:

1. Of what street gang was Edwin Ramos a member, according to Stillwell?

Cinnamon Stillwell, "San Francisco: Sanctuary City Gone Awry," SFGate.com, July 16, 2008. Reprinted by permission.

2. According to a local CBS poll cited by the author, what percentage of San Franciscans believe illegal immigrants should be turned over to proper authorities and deported?

3. As Stillwell reports, how much money per month per person does San Francisco pay to house illegal immigrant juvenile offenders in rehabilitation centers?

San Francisco's political establishment has long prided itself on providing a haven for illegal immigrants. Mayor Gavin Newsom even launched a taxpayer-funded $83,000 "public awareness campaign" earlier this year [2008] assuring illegal immigrants that the "sanctuary city" by the bay was in their court.

And indeed it is. Under the city's 1989 voter-approved sanctuary ordinance, police officers and other city employees are prohibited from inquiring into immigration status. In addition, the city will not direct municipal funds or employees towards assisting federal immigration enforcement, unless such assistance is required by federal or state law or a warrant.

Sanctuary for Murderers and Thugs

No doubt such protections warm the heart of the city's liberal leadership. But San Francisco's status as a sanctuary city is having unintended consequences.

The brutal and senseless murder last month of Tony Bologna and his sons Michael, 20, and Matthew, 16, at the hands of Edwin Ramos, a native of El Salvador and known member of the Mara Salvatrucha (MS-13) street gang, was a reminder that inviting illegal activity can turn deadly. The Bolognas were on their way back from a family picnic when they inadvertently blocked Ramos' car from making a left turn in the Excelsior district. When Bologna politely backed up to let the other car past, Ramos responded by opening fire and killing

173

all three passengers. Ramos has been charged with three counts of murder, with the added penalty of street-gang involvement.

So far, much of the outcry surrounding the case has centered on San Francisco district attorney Kamala Harris' policy of not seeking the death penalty, in this case, against the wishes of widow, Danielle Bologna. But in the process, Ramos' immigration status has largely been overlooked. Ramos' original lawyer, Joseph O'Sullivan, claimed that his client was in the country legally and applying for permanent residence, but federal immigration authorities insist otherwise and promise to deport Ramos if he is convicted. O'Sullivan has since asked to be removed from the case, claiming a connection via a previous client. Thus, he has never had to explain his assertions regarding Ramos' immigration status.

This certainly wasn't Ramos' first brush with the law. He was booked both on felony weapons charges and for being a member of a criminal street gang earlier [the same] year, but escaped prosecution for lack of evidence. However, as reported by the *San Francisco Chronicle*, the San Francisco Police Department "cited 'numerous documented contacts' that officers had with Ramos and [his companion] Lopez, and said both were active members of the MS-13 street gang.'" But thanks to San Francisco's sanctuary city status, instead of being reported to federal immigration authorities and deported, Ramos was allowed to continue to roam the streets of San Francisco until his arrest for the Bologna killings.

Moving Juvenile Felons

San Francisco's sanctuary policy has also taken a statewide toll. While adult illegal immigrant felons are not protected by the ordinance, no such stipulation exists for juvenile offenders, and city officials have used that loophole to dump the problem onto other counties. Earlier this month [July 2008], San Bernardino County officials threatened to sue the city of San Francisco for sending a group of Honduran, illegal immi-

Sanctuary Breaks Federal Law

Sanctuary Cities are in violation of Federal law [Illegal Immigration Reform Act of 1996]. That law provides that "States and localities may not adopt policies, formally or informally, that prohibit employees from communicating with DHS [Department of Homeland Security] regarding the immigration status of individuals." But in our selective pick-and-choose system of which laws to prosecute and which to ignore, there has been no attempt to date by DHS to challenge any of the "don't ask, don't tell" declared and *de facto* sanctuary cities.

Mike McGarry, Aspen (CO) Post,
August 26, 2007. www.aspenpost.net.

grant, juvenile crack dealers to group homes in the city of Yucaipa without notification. Eight of them simply walked away from the unsecured group homes and only one has been recaptured. Officials later acknowledged that this wasn't the first time San Francisco had unloaded criminal illegal immigrants onto San Bernardino County. In fact, Yucaipa has seen a rise in violent crime in accordance with the influx of foreign offenders to its group homes in recent years.

This time around, the outcry from San Bernardino officials caused Mayor Newsom to alter the city's approach to juvenile offenders. No doubt, Newsom's interest in running for governor of California, which he announced just before the controversy erupted, influenced his decision. While Newsom may find a sympathetic audience in San Francisco to his former commitment to sanctuary protections for illegal immigrants, it could prove a liability on the statewide level.

Even on a local level, there's some indication that people are getting fed up with the city's insistence on emphasizing ideology over public safety. In a local CBS poll, 79 percent of respondents agreed that San Francisco should "turn over convicted illegal immigrants for deportation."

The Cost of Sanctuary Policies

Monetary concerns are another factor. It doesn't help that Mayor Newsom and other officials bemoan the city's $338 million budget deficit, even as funds continue to pour into sustaining San Francisco's sanctuary city policies. San Francisco has spent millions of dollars housing juvenile, illegal immigrant offenders and hundreds of thousands of dollars flying them back to their countries of origin in recent years, instead of turning them over to federal immigration authorities as federal law requires. In the wake of the furor over the Honduran case and federal authorities' demand that San Francisco end the flights, the city started housing some of the dealers in youth rehabilitation centers, costing taxpayers $7,000 per month, per person.

Then there's San Francisco Supervisor and State Assembly candidate Tom Ammiano's brilliant plan to provide municipal identification cards to those who either cannot or will not obtain a state-issued driver's license—or in other words, illegal immigrants. . . . The ID program could cost up to $2.86 million in the first three years, according to a County Clerk estimate. As it turns out, Newsom's aforementioned $83,000 taxpayer-funded love letter to illegal immigrants was just the icing on the cake.

Misdirected Humanitarianism

Supporters of San Francisco's sanctuary city policies, which include members of the local faith community who inspired the original ordinance, argue that the current approach is the only humane solution. In its 2007 pledge, the New Sanctuary

Movement, describing immigration raids, stated that "We cannot in good conscience ignore such suffering and injustice." But where is the compassion for the injustice inflicted upon American citizens? Others argue that juvenile illegal immigrants deserve special treatment because they are minors. But this ignores the fact that criminal illegal immigrants and the drug cartels for whom some of them work, are aware of San Francisco's former sanctuary loophole and have taken to falsely claiming juvenile status as a result. Still, others argue that police departments need to work with illegal immigrants in the community in order to effectively tackle crime and that fears of deportation get in the way. But extending the current, chaotic state of affairs will only lead to further crime and misery, even for those within such communities.

While San Francisco's sanctuary city ordinance may have been well-intentioned, it has resulted in an untenable and anarchic situation that is taking its toll on city residents and surrounding counties alike. Providing sanctuary for law-breakers at the expense of law-abiding citizens is neither a compassionate nor a moral approach. The issue is not one of callousness towards illegal immigrants, but rather, the duty owed American citizens by their government. In some respects, every layer of the government has failed this test, but in this case, it's the local government that is absconding on its duties. And all San Francisco officials can seem to offer up is more of the same.

They don't call it the Wild West for nothing.

Periodical and Internet Sources Bibliography

The following articles have been selected to supplement the diverse views presented in this chapter.

Walter Ewing	"The Many Facets of Effective Immigration Reform," *Society*, March 2010.
Amy Frykholm	"What Kind of Reform?" *Christian Century*, June 15, 2010.
Larry Greenley	"How to Fix Illegal Immigration," *New American*, March 4, 2008.
Randall Hansen	"Immigration & Immigration Reform in the United States: An Outsider's View," *Forum*, vol. 7, no. 3, 2009.
Kerry Howley	"Get in Line!" *Reason*, October 2008.
Mark Krikorian	"Not Amnesty but Attrition," *National Review*, March 22, 2004.
Marianne Kolbasuk McGee	"A Better Way to E-Verify?" *Information Week*, March 3, 2008.
Ramesh Ponnuru	"The Immigration Impasse," *National Review*, June 7, 2010.
Peter H. Schuck	"Birthright of a Nation," *New York Times*, August 14, 2010.
Wall Street Journal	"Blame the Employers," July 17, 2009.
Armstrong Williams	"'Sanctuary Cities' Protect Murderous Illegal Aliens," *Human Events*, October 27, 2008.

OPPOSING
VIEWPOINTS®
SERIES

CHAPTER 4

Are Illegal Immigrants Treated Fairly in the United States?

Chapter Preface

On June 3, 2008, the *New York Times* posted an editorial that began:

> Someday, the country will recognize the true cost of its war on illegal immigration. We don't mean dollars, though those are being squandered by the billions. The true cost is to the national identity: the sense of who we are and what we value. It will hit us once the enforcement fever breaks, when we look at what has been done and no longer recognize the country that did it.

The *Times* insisted that the United States, a nation founded on immigration, had lost touch with its roots and had subsequently become less welcoming to those foreigners who simply wanted a chance at a better life in America. The editorial maintained that the recent flurry of federal action to round up illegal aliens and send them back to their birth nations had nothing to do with punishing people for not entering the country the "right" way. "Legal paths are clogged or do not exist. Some backlogs are so long that they are measured in decades or generations," the newspaper averred. The real aim of ousting illegal immigrants is clear, the *Times* asserted; it is to send a message "that illegal immigrants deserve no rights, mercy or hope."

Other critics who bemoan the treatment of illegal immigrants in the United States argue that the country's stance is paradoxical—even hypocritical. Writing in an October 24, 2005, article for the *Brookhaven Courier* (the news organ of Brookhaven College in Texas), staff writer Consuelo Hernandez points out that many US employers who knowingly use illegal immigrant labor exploit these immigrants for profit, ignoring the workers' needs because undocumented employees have no legal recourse. "In some cases, their human rights are not respected by their bosses, who make them work more than 80 hours a week and pay them less than minimum wage," Hernandez writes, "because they know these immigrants fear deportation and would not contact authorities." Conor Frie-derdorf, writing in the *San Bernardino Sun* in Southern Cali-fornia, concurs, stating in an April 22, 2006, article that "ille-gal immigrants are far less likely to know their rights, far less likely to report crimes against them and far less able to re-cover from being victimized."

In the following chapter, several commentators express their views on how illegal immigrants are treated in the United States. One claims that efforts to keep illegal immigrants out has led to unnecessary deaths among border crossers, and an-other believes that the restrictive policies against illegal immi-grants is informed by racism against anyone perceived as a threat to the economic well-being or the supposed cultural unity of the nation. Opponents insist that unchecked immi-gration has a negative impact on the country and the economy that cannot be ignored. They maintain that efforts to prevent illegal entry and to deport undocumented aliens are not about punishment but about respect for the law. All the viewpoints in the chapter, though, acknowledge that the problem of ille-gal immigration continues to question American values while impinging on the lives of aliens and citizens alike.

| "Migrants [have] perished as a direct
| result of border enforcement."

Border Enforcement Has Caused Migrants' Deaths

Maria Jimenez

Maria Jimenez is an organizer with the Central American Re-
source Center (CRECEN)/America Para Todos, a civil rights
group that develops programs for immigrant workers. In the fol-
lowing viewpoint, Jimenez claims that US border policies have
made it more dangerous for immigrants crossing from Mexico to
the United States. While Jimenez accepts that America would
want to protect its borders, she contends that the miles of barri-
ers and other obstacles are adding to the death toll of migrants
that try to penetrate these defenses. She condemns the US and
Mexican governments for being too unconcerned with the grow-
ing number of fatalities, and she calls upon them to adopt a
more humane method of securing their borders.

As you read, consider the following questions:

1. As the author reports, what organizations filed a petition with the Inter-American Commission on Human
   Rights in 1994 to call into question US government hu-

Maria Jimenez, "Humanitarian Crisis: Migrant Deaths at the US-Mexico Border," ACLU of San Diego and Imperial Counties, October 1, 2009. Reprinted by permission.

man rights abuses relating to the deaths of 350 people who had died in border-crossing attempts?

2. Why does Jimenez believe the Mexican government shares responsibility with the US government for border-crossing deaths?

3. According to Jimenez, how many counties on or near the US-Mexico border does the border patrol monitor?

Men, women, and children go to their deaths day after day crossing the U.S.-Mexico border. Estimates of the death toll range from 3,861 to 5,607 in the last fifteen years [1994–2009]. Immigration policies have severely restricted legal entry, and border security policies have forced unauthorized entry through dangerous routes in perilous conditions. With the implementation of the "Border National Strategic Plan for 1994 and Beyond," border and immigration policies have been organized and executed [according to a report by the Inter-American Commission on Human Rights,] "in a way that has knowingly led to the deaths of immigrants seeking to enter the United States." Migrants have faced increasingly difficult, life-threatening situations in attempts to gain entry into the United States. In his testimony before the U.S. Commission for Civil Rights, Professor Wayne Cornelius observed that these border security policies have "constituted the most obvious, the most acute, and the most systemic violation of human rights occurring on U.S. soil today."

A Human Rights Issue

Fifteen years have elapsed since the first deadly outcomes of border enforcement strategy revealed a flagrant disregard for the safety and human rights of migrants. In 1999, the American Civil Liberties Union of San Diego and Imperial Counties and the California Rural Legal Assistance Foundation challenged this wholesale abuse in a petition filed before the Inter-American Commission on Human Rights (IACHR) on behalf of 350 persons who had died in unauthorized entries into the United States during the implementation of Operation Gatekeeper [to secure California's border with Mexico in 1994]. In 2005, the IACHR ruled the petition as inadmissible for failing to exhaust domestic remedies. However, the IACHR left untouched the substantive arguments and their basis in international law. In the arguments, the petitioners established the following facts about U.S. authorities:

1. they were aware that U.S. border enforcement strategies placed migrants in mortal danger;

2. they had knowledge that migrants had perished as a direct result of border enforcement strategies; and

3. they had failed to develop any effective response to the mounting death toll.

The United States had not complied with international and human rights law acknowledging the principle of good faith, the abuse-of-rights principle and the human right to life. The petition recognized the United States' sovereign right to the use of force in protecting its national security, to control its borders, and to adopt an effective border strategy. However, when exercising that right, the United States is under the obligation to ensure that its policies and actions respect the human right to life, human integrity and human dignity. It must also act to minimize threats to physical integrity and well-being. Finally, it must guarantee its actions are proportionate, necessary, and that no other alternative is available.

A Lack of Concern

The deaths of migrants have not ceased, nor have life-threatening border policies meaningfully changed in the ten years since the filing of the petition. The United States has not changed its direction, and Mexico has become its silent partner. In 2007, Mexico's National Commission of Human Rights

Estimates of Deaths Per Fiscal Year by Source

Year	BSI	SRE plus
1994	—	23
1995	—	61
1996	—	87
1997	—	149
1998	254	329
1999	241	358
2000	372	499
2001	328	387
2002	322	371
2003	334	417
2004	328	373
2005	366	516
2006	363	485
2007	329	827
2008	320	725
2009	304	—
Total	3,861	5,607

Notes: BSI—U.S. Department of Homeland Security Border Safety Initiative
SRE plus—Mexico's Secretariat of Foreign Relations plus other news sources in Mexico

TAKEN FROM: Maria Jimenez, "Humanitarian Crisis: Migrant Deaths at the US-Mexico Border," ACLU of San Diego and Imperial Counties, October 1, 2009.

issued "*Todos Saben, Nadie Sabe*" [All Know, No One Knows], a report exposing the indifference to the tragedy of deaths unfolding daily on the U.S.-Mexico border. Conservatively, the report concludes that at least one migrant dies every day. Routine in their occurrence, these deaths have passed unnoticed and have become invisible in the public consciousness. Both the U.S. and Mexican governments have failed to acknowledge their responsibility in contributing to deaths of hundreds of migrants every year. Mexico has fallen short in its affirmative obligation to protect life by changing the economic conditions that force its citizens to migrate and confront life-threatening situations on its northern border. For its part, the United States has expanded fencing and other components of border control policies that cause these deaths.

Barriers and Fatalities Grow

Rather than spurring authorities to adjust apprehension techniques, the deaths of migrants have become an integral component of border security policies, laws, and measures to strengthen border enforcement at the U.S.-Mexico border. Securing the border from transnational threats has become the cornerstone of trade, immigration, and national security policy. Setting aside mounting evidence substantiating the fatal results of border strategies, national strategic plans for border security have continued to incorporate and build upon the 1994 national border strategy. Currently, the "2006–2010 National Strategic Plan" expands the urgency of its mission. It explicitly explains:

> ". . . the daily attempts to cross the border by thousands of illegal aliens from countries around the globe continue to present a threat to U.S. national security. Some would classify the majority of these aliens as 'economic migrants.' However, an ever-present threat exists from the potential for terrorists to employ the same smuggling and transportation networks, infrastructure, drop houses and other support and then use these masses of illegal aliens as 'cover' for a successful cross-border penetration."

In this perspective, the border enforcement strategy has been held up as a necessary weapon in defense of the homeland and the protection of the lives of its citizens. To date, the most important beneficiary of this policy justification has been the Department of Homeland Security Customs and Border Protection budget, which has expanded from $6 billion to $10.1 billion between the fiscal years FY 04 to FY 09. The bulk of these resources have been spent on strengthening border enforcement. The U.S. Border Patrol has increased in size from 18,000 to 20,000 agents. The five-year Security Border Initiative and SBInet have received infusions of technology and infrastructure to form a "virtual fence." Physical barrier and fencing mile construction has also intensified. In this national security scheme, migrant casualties are viewed as an unfortunate but necessary consequence of the global war on terrorism. . . .

Death Tolls Are Increasing

Death looms large even with the current decline in rates of job availability and apprehensions for unauthorized border crossers. The dip in the economy and arrests of undocumented migrants has not led to lower rates of death. On the contrary, most sources indicate that there has been a substantial increase in the rate of death in relation to the number of apprehensions and to the numbers for the same time period the year before. For instance, the 67 bodies recovered in Texas's McAllen Sector in 2008 represented a 72 percent increase from the 39 in 2007. In July 2009, the Mexican Consulate in Calexico, California, expressed dismay that the 17 migrants who died [that] year had already exceeded the numbers of each of the last two years. In May 2009, the *Arizona Daily Star's* comparative analysis of bodies recovered for the Yuma and Tucson Sector per 100,000 apprehensions found that the risk of dying was 1.5 times higher in 2009 than in 2004 and 17 times greater than in 1998.

An Unknown Number of Fatalities

How many persons die in unauthorized border entries into the United States from Mexican territory? This straightforward question is difficult to answer. There is no coordinated process to systemize counting the dead. Estimates vary with the source, the criteria used to identify remains as those of undocumented migrants, and the method for registering the dead.

According to the U.S. Department of Homeland Security, 390 bodies of unauthorized border crossers were recovered by the U.S. Border Patrol in the federal fiscal year FY 08 (October 1, 2007 to September 30, 2008). These are bodies or remains found within the 45 counties on or near the U.S.-Mexico border ... or cases where the Border Patrol was involved. The tally does not take into account cases in which local authorities are the first to respond to calls of humanitarian organizations, border residents or other migrants. By excluding these known deaths, the Border Patrol figures are the least complete. Comparisons of Border Patrol counts to those compiled by the Pima County [Arizona] Medical Examiner's Office (PCMEO) resulted in significant differences by 44 bodies/ remains (32 percent) in 2002, by 56 (43 percent) in 2003, and by 46 (35.6 percent) in 2004. According to the *Arizona Daily Star's* database, in 2009 the discrepancies persisted between Border Patrol and Arizona medical examiners' records of unauthorized border crosser recovered bodies from 2005 to April 2009. It also does not include the bodies or remains of migrants who may have been injured in the United States but made their way back to Mexico, who may have drowned in a river, canal, or ocean but whose corpses were deposited by currents on the Mexican side or who are classified as locals by Mexican authorities.

> "The standard culprit [for border-crossing deaths] in polite opinion—the Border Patrol—is not only blameless, but spends much of its time rescuing helpless illegals, saving thousands of lives."

Border Enforcement Is Not to Blame for Migrants' Deaths

Mark Krikorian

In the following viewpoint, Mark Krikorian claims that the US Border Patrol is not responsible for the deaths of immigrants crossing the US-Mexico border. In fact, he asserts, the border patrol has often saved the lives of those crossing the border. Instead, Krikorian blames the economy and the American lifestyle for attracting immigrants, and he criticizes the government for being lax on finding and deporting aliens already in America—a paradox that only encourages more immigrants to make the dangerous journey across the border. Mark Krikorian is the executive director of the Center for Immigration Studies, an independent, nonpartisan, nonprofit research organization.

Mark Krikorian, "Long, Hot Summer," *National Review Online*, June 9, 2006. Reprinted by permission.

As you read, consider the following questions:

1. As Krikorian explains, what has forced many illegal immigrants to make the border-crossing journey through dangerous, less-populated areas where water is scarce and temperatures are high?

2. According to Krikorian, by what percentage had work-site arrests of illegal immigrants fallen between 1999 and 2003?

3. In the author's view, what other pressing emergency seems to be superseding Americans' concern about the plight of illegal immigrants?

This week [of June 4–10, 2006,] marked the start of the season for media features on illegal aliens dying in the desert. The *Washington Post*'s entry on Tuesday [June 6] was especially horrific, telling of a blameless three-year-old boy who died of dehydration and exposure as he accompanied his mother across the border. *Sixty Minutes*, meanwhile, reran on Sunday a more policy-oriented offering, but pegged it to the death of 18-year-old Abran Gonzales, "a quiet kid. He never hurt anybody. He just wanted to work and come back home."

The message of these stories, and the cascade of other stories we will see from the mainstream media over the next few months, is that such tragedies are the result of increased border enforcement, which, in the *Post* reporter's words, "funneled them onto increasingly perilous trails where temperatures are high, water is scarce and danger is abundant."

It's true, of course, that the concentration of enforcement resources near the urban areas of San Diego and El Paso over the past decade or so shifted the crossing patterns to more remote areas, especially to the Arizona desert. And while it's not clear that the total number of border deaths has actually increased (since many people were killed in traffic accidents and criminal assaults during the chaotic years when those two cities were the focus of illegal crossings), the human toll is real, and heartrending.

Border Patrol Is Blameless

But are tighter border controls really the cause? Is elite opinion right in implying that we, as a nation, are responsible for the deaths of these people by trying to control our borders? If so, then perhaps the supporters of open borders are right and American sovereignty is itself a crime.

Fortunately not.

Many people share culpability for these deaths. The illegals themselves, of course, are moral agents and responsible for their actions (including endangering their children—how, unless you're fleeing certain death, can you justify risking the life of a three-year-old in a trackless wasteland?). The smugglers, many of them scum of the earth, not infrequently abandon their charges to the vultures. And the thieving elites of Mexico and the other dysfunctional societies in Latin America also share the burden.

Interestingly, the standard culprit in polite opinion—the Border Patrol—is not only blameless, but spends much of its time rescuing helpless illegals, saving thousands of lives.

We, as Americans, do share responsibility, but not in the way that fashionable thinking would have you believe. It's not border enforcement, as such, that's at fault, but rather the toxic combination of tough (or at least tougher) border enforcement with easy access to jobs.

The Lure of the Easy Life

The job magnet is strong because few businesses are ever punished for hiring illegals, making the opportunities in America worth the risk of the dangerous crossing. The amount of investigative time devoted to worksite enforcement of immigration laws fell steadily from 1999 to 2003, dropping by more

Border Patrol Agents Respond to Immigrant Distress Calls

On Sunday [July 12, 2009], BORSTAR [Border Search, Trauma and Rescue] agents responded to a 911 call of three individuals lost in the mountains north of Nogales, Ariz. The caller stated they had been lost for over a day since crossing the International Border. Agents were able to gather all necessary information from the caller to make a successful rescue of the three individuals near Arivaca, Ariz. None of the individuals required medical attention. All individuals were determined to be illegal aliens and transported to the Tucson Processing Center.

As the temperatures reach into triple digits the men and woman of the Tucson Sector Border Patrol, along with their law enforcement counterparts stand ready as guardians of our Nations Borders from all threats. However, at a moment's notice agents can take on the responsibility of providing humanitarian aid to those in need, most of the time it is for those who have fallen victim to smugglers who leave them behind in the desert.

US Customs and Border Protection, press release,
July 16, 2009.

than half, according to the GAO [Government Accountability Office]. The number of worksite arrests fell by 84 percent. And, from 1999 to 2004, the number of fines issued to employers fell by 99 percent, plummeting to a laughable nationwide total of three.

Only in the past six months, after a quarter century of scorched-earth resistance from open-borders advocates, have the two houses of Congress separately voted to require businesses to verify the Social Security numbers of new hires—and it still may not come to pass because of irreconcilable differences in the bills.

And it's not just jobs. The government at all levels has taken many actions over the past few years to make life easier for illegal aliens—the Treasury Department signaling to banks that Mexico's illegal-alien ID card is an acceptable credential for opening bank accounts; legislatures offering in-state tuition subsidies to illegals attending state universities; and city councils barring local police from using immigration law in the course of their duties.

In other words, we've told prospective illegal aliens that they'll have to risk their lives to get in, but once they're clear of the border, they're home free. With government establishing that kind of incentive structure, it's a wonder more people don't die in the desert.

Sending Mixed Messages

While no one is pleased by the deaths, Americans like the idea that foreigners are willing to take such risks to get into our country. At a time when the ties that bind us as a people are increasingly frayed and Muslim fanatics plot to nuke us, we take some consolation in the fact that many outsiders still want to come here to live. As [then] Gov. George W. Bush (quoted in *Boy Genius*) said of a remote and treacherous part of the Texas border, "Hell, if they'll walk across Big Bend, we want 'em."

But as a civilized people, we must face up to our responsibility for the border deaths and stop sending mixed messages. We face two morally consistent choices: on the one hand, we can continue to ignore worksite enforcement, but open the borders. This would bring our interior and border strategies in sync and stop forcing aliens to cross in remote and deadly areas. It would also mean the dissolution of the American republic.

Or, we can get serious about upholding the law *everywhere* in our country, combining strong border controls with muscular interior enforcement. This means not only more arrests and deportations, but also a comprehensive firewall strategy that would bar illegals from access to important institutions of our society—no jobs, no bank accounts, no driver's licenses, no car loans, no mortgages.

By ending the mixed messages we send illegals, we can fundamentally change the incentives they face, and the decisions they make. In this way, American people can both protect the nation's sovereignty and minimize these tragic deaths at the same time.

> *"There are many reasons to be con-*
> *cerned with the rate of illegal immigra-*
> *tion in this country. But at the very*
> *roots of this 'nativist' movement, there*
> *is some very real racism."*

Many Anti-Immigration Protesters Have Racist Motives

Devona Walker

Devona Walker is the senior financial and political reporter for the Loop21.com, a website providing economic, political, and cultural news and opinion on topics relating to the African American community. In the viewpoint that follows, she insists that some anti-immigration groups have racist motives for their opposition to immigration. According to Walker, members of the Americans for Legal Immigration Political Action Committee (ALIPAC) have recently been accused of inciting violence at pro-immigration rallies by inviting skinhead groups to protest at these assemblies.

As you read, consider the following questions:

1. What is the "papers please" legislation that Walker condemns?

Devona Walker, "Anti-Immigration Movement Steeped in Racism: Here's the Proof," TheLoop21.com, May 21, 2010. Reprinted by permission.

2. According to the author, what "permit game" did Dan Smeriglio play to intentionally bring skinheads in contact with pro-immigration demonstrators?

3. What children's television cartoon character has been used by anti-immigration groups as a poster child for the supposed crime of border crossing, according to Walker?

Anyone who criticizes Arizona's immigration law [SB 1070, signed into law on April 23, 2010], requiring that law enforcement stop anyone they suspect of being an undocumented or illegal immigrant, has been criticized—accused of playing the race card or race-baiting.

There are many reasons to be concerned with the rate of illegal immigration in this country. But at the very roots of this "nativist" movement, there is some very real racism.

Don't believe me, then perhaps you might take the word of one of the nation's most vehemently anti-immigrant lobbying groups, ALIPAC (Americans for Legal Immigration Political Action Committee).

Inviting Trouble

ALIPAC was recently forced to withdraw their support from a rally in Arizona supporting SB 1070, otherwise known as the "papers please" legislation, because they found out that its organizers were not only welcoming but inviting racist skinhead groups to the protest.

"We are sad to announce that ALIPAC is withdrawing support for any rallies in Arizona in June [2010] to support SB 1070 due to the discovery of racist group involvement and the actions of former Congressman Tom Tancredo [Colorado]," ALIPAC said in a written statement, one that I originally found on the white supremacist website amren.com. "We take our commitment to working with and unifying Americans of every race and walk of life behind the effort to secure our

Tancredo Says Immigrants Must Assimilate

Previous generations of immigrants had to come a long way to get to the United States. The option of returning home for something like a family gathering wasn't an option. They had to completely embrace America and the notion of becoming an American. Most of today's immigrants take a much shorter trip to get here, and live close enough to their country of origin that they can go home for the weekend. . . . The pressure to assimilate that [President Theodore] Roosevelt recognized as so critical at the turn of the 20th century has nearly disappeared in some cities here in the 21st. If we do not demand that immigrants get into the great melting pot—if immigrants are permitted to continue to form their own independent cultural, political and linguistic enclaves—if we fail to instill in new arrivals the language, culture, and values that bind America together as a nation, we will soon cease to have a nation.

Tom Tancredo, Human Events, *December 14, 2006.*

borders very seriously. While the illegal alien supporters constantly make false accusations of racism and racist involvement, it is of paramount importance that groups like ours work to keep any racist element out of our events and operations."

ALIPAC speaks specifically about the organizer Dan Smeriglio. Smeriglio runs an anti–illegal immigration group called the "Voice of the People" but he is directly associated with various skinhead groups, most notably Keystone United, formerly Keystone State "Skinheads" (KSS). Its membership has, in the past, also been members of more violent groups such as the Ku Klux Klan [KKK] and Aryan Nations. One of its members, Steve Smith, who was previously affiliated with the KKK and Aryan Nations, was arrested in 2003 along with two other KSS members—Keith Carney and Steve Monteforte—for assaulting a black man in Scranton, PA. Back in November [2009], several members of the North Eastern PA Chapter of Keystone United attended a local Tea Party Against Amnesty. This event was also hosted by Smeriglio.

"All in all, I must say the event was a success for Keystone United. We had the opportunity to speak with new people and gave them some literature and newsletters. We also had the privilege to meet and talk to a gentleman all the way from Europe. He explained to us how European countries are facing the same issues of Illegal Immigration as we are here in the U.S.," the Keystone Skinheads said in a written statement about attending the event.

Protesting Without Permits

But it's not just Smeriglio's associations that are troubling, it's his tactics of intentionally trying to set up an environment that will incite violence. Let's call it the permit game. Smeriglio routinely, according to ALIPAC, invited them and other anti–illegal immigration groups and activists to events telling them they had obtained permits to protest at a particular site. But in each case, it was a lie. Immigrant support groups and people actually had the permits to protest at those locations.

So, how does this work? He intentionally invites the racist fringe to come to anti-illegal immigration rallies, then he lies and tells them they are supposed to protest where the pro-immigrant groups are protesting.

The guy's intent is obvious: He wants a violent altercation.

"A few weeks ago, we got behind a rally in Phoenix on June 5 being planned by Dan Smeriglio of Voice of The People USA and retired Congressman Tom Tancredo. On Monday, May 10th, we discovered two painful truths that forced us to take a new direction," ALIPAC wrote. "First, June 5 organizer Dan Smeriglio had radically misinformed us about his possession of permits for a location in Phoenix on June 5. He did not have any permits and the illegal alien supporter had permits for the location he had promised us. This happened last year when Smeriglio promised us he had permits for a rally in [Washington,] DC and we had to cancel when we learned he had misinformed us and the illegal alien supporters had the permit for our rally location. Unfortunately we had quite a case of political déjà vu with Mr. Smeriglio misleading organization leaders about permits, while our opposition held the ground he promised us."

The second problem also arose around June 5, when we picked up a release by a smaller illegal alien supporting group called One People's Project. The group was attacking Dan Smeriglio claiming he was working with skinheads and Nazis and attacking ALIPAC for associating with Smeriglio. "However, we reviewed the video and computer screen shots that our opposition possesses regarding Dan Smeriglio and discovered that they are correct. The video and screen shots of Dan Smeriglio's Facebook account indicates that he has willingly been working with members of racist skinhead groups long after he knew their identities and politics." . . .

Teaching the Wrong Lessons

Now the anti–illegal immigration folks are disparaging Dora the Explorer—they are upset that she is teaching little American children Spanish, and they have decided to claim that she is an illegal immigrant and have posted a mugshot of her on the Internet. In her police mugshot, the doe-eyed cartoon heroine with the bowl haircut has a black eye, battered lip and bloody nose. Dora the Explorer's alleged crime? "Illegal Border Crossing [and] Resisting Arrest."

"Dora is kind of like a blank screen onto which people can project their thoughts and feelings about Latinos," said

Erynn Masi de Casanova, a sociology professor at the University of Cincinnati. "They feel like they can say negative things because she's only a cartoon character." Now, come on! I am not a huge fan of Dora either, but only because her unchaperoned adventures seem a bit reckless, but an illegal immigrant? Please! If these folks are already racially profiling cartoon characters, what do you think they will do to real world Hector and Jose?

> "What those playing the race card seem to be missing is that much of the resentment isn't aimed at Latinos, or even illegal immigrants—but at the employers who abuse our broken immigration laws."

Opposition to Illegal Immigration Is Not a Racial Issue

Clayton E. Cramer

In the following viewpoint, Clayton E. Cramer refutes accusations that those calling for reform of illegal immigration are racists. Cramer contends that many critics are justly fearful that an unchecked influx of low-skill immigrants drives down the wages of the lowest-paid Americans and drains health care services. He claims these opponents are driven by an urge to reform legislation, not exact revenge upon blameless immigrants. In his view, new laws should punish employers who knowingly hire illegal aliens and thus encourage immigrants to cross the borders without pursuing proper immigration channels. Clayton E. Cramer is

Clayton E. Cramer, "Racism and Illegal Immigration," Pajamas Media, June 17, 2009. Reprinted by permission.

a software engineer and historian. He has published six books, including Armed America: The Remarkable Story of How and Why Guns Became as American as Apple Pie.

As you read, consider the following questions:

1. How does Cramer portray the skill and education levels of most illegal immigrants?

2. According to the author, who pays for the health care illegal immigrants receive in America?

3. What percentage of the uninsured in America comprises illegal immigrants, as Cramer reports?

I'm quite tired of the constant accusation that opponents of illegal immigration are racists.

[San Diego *Union Tribune* editorial board member] Ruben Navarrette's [June 8, 2009,] PJM [Pajamas Media] column uses a sample size of *one reader* to determine that racism is the real reason that Americans are concerned. He claims that what most Americans actually *say*—that it's "about respect for law and order and worry over how illegal immigrants supposedly take jobs, drain services, pollute the environment, wreck the schools, and diminish quality of life"—is just a sham. It's *really* about racism and fear of living in a Latino nation.

Criticism Targets Laws Not People

I have no illusions that racism has completely disappeared. I do—occasionally—hear anti-Hispanic sentiments expressed. But the claim that the average American is afraid of Latinos outbreeding us shows a level of long-term thinking that I find laughable. What those playing the race card seem to be missing is that much of the resentment isn't aimed at Latinos, or even illegal immigrants—but at the employers who abuse our broken immigration laws.

Illegal immigrants are overwhelmingly low-skilled and poorly educated. What they do have is a willingness to work

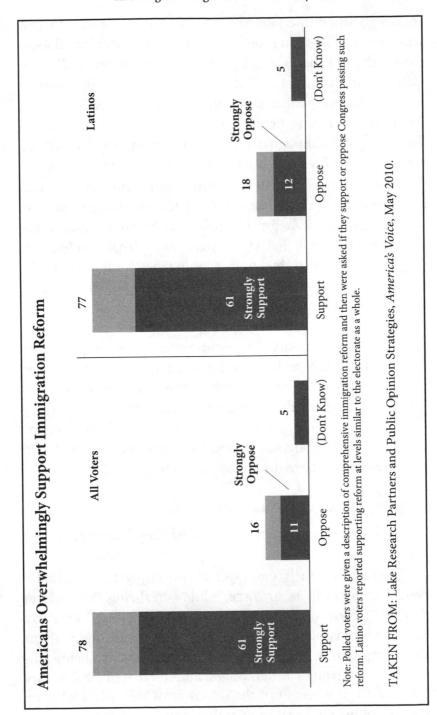

Americans Overwhelmingly Support Immigration Reform

All Voters

78

Support

61
Strongly
Support

16

Oppose

11

Strongly
Oppose

5

(Don't Know)

Latinos

77

Support

61
Strongly
Support

18

Oppose

12

Strongly
Oppose

5

(Don't Know)

Note: Polled voters were given a description of comprehensive immigration reform and then were asked if they support or oppose Congress passing such reform. Latino voters reported supporting reform at levels similar to the electorate as a whole.

TAKEN FROM: Lake Research Partners and Public Opinion Strategies, *America's Voice*, May 2010.

and to go where the jobs are—and that isn't Mexico. In that sense, we may be seeing some of Mexico's best. But that doesn't change the fact that increasing the supply of laborers, all other factors being constant, *will* drive down wages in that market segment. In my market segment, software engineering, cheap Asian labor coming here on H-1B [work] visas has driven down wages—although I don't expect many of you will be sympathetic if I tell you what those diminished wage rates are!

However, unskilled illegal immigrants who have flooded across our Southern border the last few years aren't driving down the wages of well-paid professionals. They are lowering the wages for unskilled U.S. citizens and legal residents. It might not be much, but even a dollar per hour matters for people who earn hardly above minimum wage. For some, it's the difference between self-sufficiency and needing government assistance.

In addition, because illegal immigrants are poorly paid, they are less likely to have health insurance than the average American. So what happens when they need medical care? Like many others without health insurance, they delay seeking help until it is an emergency, and the costs of those emergency room visits are shouldered by taxpayers or cost-shifted to those who do have insurance.

Blaming Unscrupulous Employers

Let me be very clear: I am not blaming illegal immigrants for this.

I'm blaming their employers, who enjoy the *individual* benefit of a cheap labor force, while socializing the costs of that labor force onto the rest of us. If the Republican Party had any brains, it would be banging the drum loudly about this—emphasizing that the poorest Americans are being impoverished through lower wages and increased health care costs, all for the benefit of the minority of employers who are knowingly hiring illegal immigrants.

If the Democratic Party had any integrity, it would recognize that part of why we have the staggering 43 million uninsured Americans is illegal immigrants—who make up 15 percent of the uninsured. I don't hold out much hope that enforcing our immigration laws will *dramatically* increase wages for the least-skilled Americans, but there *are* Americans right how who can't *quite* afford health insurance—and who probably could if they weren't competing with the eleven million illegal immigrants that were in the U.S. in 2006.

Rewarding Illegal Immigration

If the U.S. had severe labor shortages right now, I suppose that I would be a bit more sympathetic to guest worker programs or to a path to legal residence for illegal immigrants. But with the unemployment rate in May hitting 9.4 percent—and the San Francisco Federal Reserve Bank warning that it could hit 11 percent before the jobs come back—it is lunacy to consider any strategy that rewards illegal immigrants, either those already here or those considering crossing the border. It is especially crazy when you consider that the Americans with whom illegal immigrants largely compete for jobs are the least likely to have a savings account to help them through months (or years) of unemployment.

The chattering classes don't seem to ever quite understand this concern about illegal immigration and jobs. I suspect that if English-speaking India were right next door—and newspapers, schools, and universities were run by unscrupulous sorts who didn't ask too many questions before hiring workers— journalists, teachers, and professors would suddenly understand the concern. Or at least they would shortly after all three professions started paying minimum wage—with no benefits.

> "As the US economy worsens, places that welcomed—if not courted—inexpensive labor during the 1990s economic boom have reversed course."

The Economic Downturn Has Changed Many Americans' Views of Illegal Immigrants

Lawrence Hardy

In the following viewpoint, Lawrence Hardy explores the reactions of pro- and anti-immigrant camps in Prince William County, Virginia, after the passage of a local resolution allowing police officers to ask any detainee for proof of legal residency status. As Hardy reports, supporters of this resolution argue that it will rid the community of immigrants feeding off the system and draining tax dollars; opponents believe it cuts tax revenue and keeps vitally needed immigrant worker money from enriching local businesses and services. Many residents' views of illegal immigrants have changed with the economic downturn, the author notes. Hardy specifically focuses on the concerns of school teachers and board members who believe educators have a duty to teach all students—regardless of their legal status—and the fears

Lawrence Hardy, "The Divided Line," *American School Board Journal*, September 2008. Reprinted with permission from American School Board Journal, September 2008.

of immigrant parents who just want their children to learn without worry of deportation. Lawrence Hardy is a senior editor at the American School Board Journal.

As you read, consider the following questions:

1. As Hardy reports, what negative reactions did Prince William County residents have toward illegal immigrants once the housing bubble burst?

2. What percentage of the total school enrollment in Prince William County comprised English for Speakers of Other Languages students in 2007, according to the author?

3. According to Corey Stewart, as cited by Hardy, the Prince William County resolution was responsible for a decrease in what four immigrant-related problems?

She hasn't told her 7-year-old, but how could the boy not know? He's a bright child, after all, and as a Head Start student in Prince William County, Va., he had translated for his teacher and other children even though he'd only been away from Mexico for three years.

The boy asks his mother about the monitoring bracelet around his father's ankle. He knows she is scared. He sees the family's belongings, packed in cardboard boxes and bulging black trash bags, and knows change is coming.

"At the beginning, when we moved here, everything was different," the boy's mother, a small, soft-spoken woman, says through an interpreter. "But now, things have gotten very tough."

Tough because of the immigration raid that resulted in her husband's arrest. Tough because, as of mid-June [2008], the family did not know if they could remain in this country. And tough because many Prince William residents have stated publicly that people like them should go back to their own country.

As the US economy worsens, places that welcomed—if not courted—inexpensive labor during the 1990s economic boom have reversed course. Undocumented workers, who have no real home, are now targets.

This is true in Prince William County, an exurb of Washington, D.C., that has been at the center of a firestorm since last fall [2007], when its Board of Supervisors adopted a resolution allowing police to check the immigration status of persons detained for even minor violations of state or municipal law.

"Wait and See" Approach

Chairman Corey A. Stewart has made national headlines, boasting that sometimes he has to "play hardball" on immigration issues and calling localities to which hundreds of families are fleeing "sanctuary counties."

The unrest presents ongoing challenges for the 73,000-student school district, which must educate an increasingly diverse population while being careful not to antagonize the county board that funds more than half of its operating budget. The district's leadership, from the board to the superintendent, has been largely silent on the issue.

"None of them is going to go out on a limb and say anything that's the least bit critical of Corey Stewart," says Lucy Beauchamp, who retired in 2007 after 16 years on the school board, 14 as chairwoman.

Beauchamp says the district is taking a "wait and see" approach, hoping to learn, for example, if some of the hundreds of immigrant children who left the system—either because of the resolution or economic conditions—will return in the fall.

"More than anything right now," Beauchamp says, "there is a [question of], 'How will this affect our schools?' They don't know."

A Polarized Community

Americans may be divided on what, if any, services illegal immigrants should receive, but the law is clear: Public schools must educate all students, documented or not. But that is made tougher when your community is as polarized as Prince William.

Starting in the 1990s, the county reaped the rewards of an unprecedented housing boom, fueled by newcomers looking for cheaper (and often larger) homes than they could find in neighboring Fairfax County. Homes were built largely with immigrant labor, documented and undocumented, from places like Mexico and El Salvador.

As the boom continued, laborers and their families moved in too, flocking to apartment complexes lining Jefferson Davis Highway and other neighborhoods where they could find affordable housing.

Then the construction bubble burst. Gas prices spiked, making the long commute to Washington more expensive. Housing values dropped precipitously and foreclosures soared. Residents complained about immigrants ruining their neighborhoods, saying they were crowding into single-family houses and apartments, littering and making noise, and congregating in 7-Eleven parking lots while waiting to be picked up for construction jobs that were increasingly hard to find.

The supervisors' resolution resulted in an uproar. Proponents praised supervisors for standing up to illegal immigrants who had turned the county, in the words of one resident, into "North Mexico." On the other side, immigrant advocates said Prince William had dealt itself a devastating blow.

"It sends the message that it is OK to target these people, and we are going to have to live with this message for decades," says Dexter Fox, chairman of Unity in the Community, a county group. "And that's a tragedy."

A Lose-Lose Situation

What do school leaders think about the situation? It's hard to tell, because most are saying as little as possible. Only one of the eight board members, Gilbert A. Trenum Jr., talked to *ASBJ* [*American School Board Journal*] for this story, and he was careful not to comment on the resolution.

"Our focus is on educating all the students who come though our doors," Trenum says.

The district should make up the loss of 1,200 students this past school year—600 of them English language learners—and even grow slightly this fall, Trenum says. Far more serious, in financial terms, is the 15-percent drop in residential property values.

"We are more dependent on our residential housing market than some of the other counties," Trenum says. "We don't have the commercial tax base that some of the surrounding counties have."

At the controversy's height, Superintendent Steven L. Walts and others spoke on Spanish-language radio, emphasizing that all immigrant children were safe—and welcome—in the public schools. But when contacted by *ASBJ*, the superintendent would only speak through a prepared statement.

"We are pleased to welcome all students in our community to school every day," the statement reads. "The Prince William Public School System is committed to providing a World-Class Education for all students."

Paul Houston, who recently retired as executive director of the American Association of School Administrators, says the district faces a lose-lose situation.

"If the superintendent or board said something about it, they could risk losing money—and still have the problem" with the local government, Houston says. "It's a very difficult position for these folks."

Frank E. Barham, executive director of the Virginia School Boards Association, says it's not the board's job to discuss the resolution because members weren't involved in debating or voting on it.

"I can understand why Prince William is not commenting because it's not their dog, directly, in this fight," Barham says. "They may have personal opinions, but the corporate opinion is, 'I've got to educate every child who lives here.'"

Confrontations on Local Resolutions

The pickup truck's bumper stickers leave no doubt as to the driver's views: "*No Mas Illegals.*" "*What part of 'Illegal' do you not understand!*" "*Anmista, No. Deportacion, Si.*" One has a silhouette of a lanky man falling backwards from a truck, his arms raised and sombrero flying.

The truck is parked in mid-April on one of the outlying lots of the county administrative complex. The lots are overflowing for a public hearing on the proposal by incoming Supervisor Frank Principi to rescind the controversial anti-illegal immigrant resolution.

The resolution's opponents say the measure backfired, sparking criticism from around the country. They point to millions in unanticipated costs, including overtime for law enforcement and increased crowding in the local jail.

Proponents also have come out in force. Walking to the hearing, overflowing with people and already in progress, a visitor can hear a man's voice on the loudspeaker outside, lambasting timid national politicians, ensconced some 40 miles up the road in Washington, for failing to confront illegal immigration.

"Our country is selling us out," says another resident. "Our citizens are a bunch of followers."

The resolution's critics, like Jean Mitcho, point to its effect on the community. "This county's been so polarized by this issue that no one listens to anyone else," she says. "I believe this is morally wrong and socially and economically disastrous."

Making Children Feel Welcome

Like many growing districts, Prince William has seen an unprecedented jump in diversity as enrollment has increased. More than 100 languages now are spoken in the schools, says Carol Bass, the district's supervisor for ESOL (English for Speakers of Other Languages) and World Languages. In September 2007, the district had more than 13,000 ESOL students—18 percent of the total enrollment.

Bass is enthusiastic about the district's plans to create an environment that is as diverse and cosmopolitan as the student body. Four elementary schools offer Spanish instruction, two have French, and plans call for introducing Chinese and Japanese when funds become available.

Bass says the district doesn't know whether the loss of immigrant students is attributable to the resolution—later amended to require immigration status inquiries on all arrests—or due to the economic downturn. Asked what she thinks of the resolution, she pauses before replying: "I don't have an opinion."

But, she adds, the schools cannot concern themselves with the law.

"We never lose sight of our goal," she says. "For us, that never changes, regardless of what happens politically, regardless of what happens economically. We are here to protect the right of children to feel safe and welcome at school."

Consequences of Expelling Illegals

Two weeks later, in Regina Lawlor's sixth-grade social studies class at Godwin Middle School, students are reading about Cesar Chavez and the United Farm Workers movement, which advocated for migrant workers' rights.

Lawlor asks if the children see parallels between the Central Valley of California 40 years ago and Northern Virginia today.

"In my community of townhouses, about every two houses there's a house where Hispanics used to live and it's empty," one student says.

Home foreclosures have steadily risen in Prince William; the county and nearby Prince George's County, Md., have the highest rates in the region.

"The problem is that the economy is weak and these jurisdictions need all of the positive juice they can get," says Stephen Fuller, director of the Center for Regional Analysis at George Mason University, speaking on a video sponsored by a pro-immigrant group. "In Prince William they made it worse by targeting a portion of their low-income population, making it feel less welcome. They took that spending power, that tax-generating power, that economic benefit out of the solution."

Corey Stewart, the supervisors' chairman, sees it differently. At a Capitol Hill forum in July, Stewart said the law dramatically reduced crime and the number of overcrowded houses. The drop in ESOL students will save the county money, he said, crowding in medical facilities is being eased due to a big reduction in the number of nonpaying and self-paying hospital patients—including "a virtual elimination of births by illegal immigrant women."

"We have taken our neighborhoods back," Stewart said during the forum.

A report issued at the end of July seemed to support Stewart's position. The Center for Immigration Studies, a Washington, D.C.–based think tank that supports tighter restrictions on all forms of immigration, said the number of illegal immigrants fell from 12.5 million in August 2007 to 11.2 million in May 2008—an 11 percent drop. The reports cited the, [George W.] Bush administration's support of aggressive workplace raids, which led to the detention of 400 workers at a meatpacking plant in Postville, Iowa, and tougher enforcement of immigration laws as the cause.

In Congress, Latino lawmakers are trying to put a stop to the raids until new immigration policies can be put in place. They say the human cost is too great, an opinion echoed by Beauchamp, the former school board chair.

"We believe some families are just holding their children out of school because they're frightened," Beauchamp says, noting the students are the ones who suffer. "And that's the part that I find so sad."

Fear of Deportation

Teresita Jacinto is a fifth-grade ESOL teacher and a member of the pro-immigrant group Mexicans Without Borders. As far back as last fall, families came to her class to say goodbye, claiming they were afraid to stay in Prince William. One family left for southern Virginia but didn't enroll their children for two months because they were undocumented and afraid they would be caught.

Another boy, who is still in Jacinto's class, went from being a class clown to someone who is gloomy and remote. Jacinto attributed it to early adolescent blues until she spoke with his mother, an illegal immigrant.

"He cries every morning before he goes off to school," the boy's mother told her. "Every morning my fifth-grader clings to me and cries and says, 'Mommy, I love you, I'm afraid I will never see you again.'"

Ira Mehlman, national media director of the Federation for American Immigration Reform, has heard these stories and is not swayed. The group supports wide-ranging efforts to secure the borders and stop illegal immigration.

"When you break the law, it has consequences for your family," he says. "It's not the law's fault; it's your fault."

Mehlman draws a parallel between Prince William's law and a situation in which a person refuses to pay federal income taxes and blames the "big bad IRS" for scaring his family. "Basically," he says, "what they're saying is that children should be human shields."

Feeling Like They Do Not Belong

The boy's father was arrested last spring during a raid on the construction company where he worked. He was released after three days and ordered to wear the monitoring bracelet. When a reporter visited in June, a court order had restricted the father's movements outside the home to the hours of 6 a.m. to 7 p.m. That allowed him to work, but the jobs he found lasted only two or three days.

The small apartment, which family members owned, was in foreclosure. They were preparing to move into a room at a relative's house outside Prince William County, but the boy's mother hoped they could return before school starts.

Teacher Kathy Clark says the mother was a model volunteer at her son's Head Start program and was especially good at helping children with special needs. Clark calls her "a natural teacher," and says she even won the program's top volunteer award for her efforts.

"He's obviously a smart little boy and well cared for by his mom and dad," Clark says of the child, who likes video games and basketball and wants to be a veterinarian because he likes taking care of his dog when it's sick.

In preschool, the boy brought in snapshots of his family's recent trip to Washington, D.C., and the National Mall. There he stood outside the White House, by the Lincoln Memorial, beside the Washington Monument.

If the authorities won't let him go to school, the family will return to Mexico, his mother says. She doesn't understand that federal law grants her son the right to a public school education, regardless of his parents' immigration status.

Like other immigrants in Prince William, she is afraid to leave the house and limits her trips. When she goes to the grocery store, she gets looks that she never did before.

"What are you doing here?" they seem to say. "You don't belong here."

Periodical and Internet Sources Bibliography

The following articles have been selected to supplement the diverse views presented in this chapter.

César Cuauhtémoc and García Hernández	"No Human Being Is Illegal," *Monthly Review: An Independent Socialist Magazine*, June 2008.
Nicole Weisensee Egan, Diane Herbst, Ivory Jeff Clinton	"A Town Torn Apart," *People*, September 8, 2008.
Larry Elder	"How Does Mexico Treat Its Illegals," *Human Events*, April 10, 2006.
John Garvey	"The Good Place," *Commonweal*, August 17, 2007.
Melissa Harris-Lacewell	"Believing in Justice, Blaming the Victim," *Nation*, May 31, 2010.
Roberto Lovato	"Juan Crow in Georgia," *Nation*, May 26, 2008.
Debbie Nathan	"Border Death Backstory," *Nation*, March 31, 2008.
Frank Rich	"If Arizona Were Only the Real Problem," *New York Times*, May 2, 2010.
Jesse Walker	"Exploitation or Expulsion," *Reason*, August 2006.

For Further Discussion

Chapter 1

1. According to Michael E. Telzrow, illegal immigrants are a burden on the US economy and social welfare systems. John Price, on the other hand, insists that American businesses utilize illegal immigrants to keep the costs of goods affordable for all Americans, and he refutes the notion that these undocumented individuals are a drain on social welfare. Select one aspect of the debate shared by both authors and decide whose opinion you find more convincing. Explain why you side with that author and then address why you are not convinced by the counterargument.

2. What argumentative strategy does Roger D. McGrath employ to make his claim that illegal aliens are increasing crime rates in the United States? What type of argument does Tom Barry use to refute that notion? Does the type of argument utilized by one author lead you to believe his assertions over those of the opposing view? If so, explain how; if not, why not?

3. Both Roger D. McGrath and Leo W. Banks claim that Americans should be fearful of some illegal immigrants because of the recorded crimes they have committed especially in border communities. Do you think the fears raised about illegal immigrants are justified? What evidence can you cite from any of the last four viewpoints in this chapter to substantiate your position?

Chapter 2

1. Jeff Lukens asserts that building and strengthening a physical barrier between the United States and Mexico is

an important first step to deter illegal immigrants from crossing the border. Peter Schrag contends that focusing on a physical barrier masks the real problems with current US immigration policy. How much emphasis do you think should be placed on erecting and maintaining a border fence? Explain why you believe this.

2. Arizona Law SB 1070 has garnered a fair share of media attention since it was passed in April 2010. Some have viewed it as a necessary step to round up illegal immigrants, while others believe it is a dangerous form of racial profiling. Find the text of the law online and read it. Explain whether you believe the law is appropriate or goes too far in countering the problem of illegal immigration.

Chapter 3

1. Raúl Hinojosa-Ojeda insists that a general amnesty for illegal aliens who have resided in America for many years would be a boon for the economy and national tax revenues. Hinojosa-Ojeda claims that by keeping these people in hiding, the government is losing out on their potentially greater contributions to American society. Paul Belien points out, though, that European countries who have tried amnesty never resolve the problem of illegal immigration and, in fact, attract more illegal immigrants because these aliens assume that they will earn an amnesty if they just stay in the country long enough. What do you think about this issue? Is amnesty a worthwhile antidote to the problem? Explain why or why not.

2. Jim Harper disapproves of the E-Verify method of keeping illegal immigrants from gaining employment and thus deterring them from entering the country. Harper argues that the system will unintentionally discourage employers from hiring anyone Hispanic to avoid the costs of using

E-Verify and taking the chance that the worker is undocumented. Do you think this argument is valid? Explain why
or why not.

3. Sanctuary programs are one example of local
   communities' providing their own policies to deal with
   some of the issues related to illegal immigration in response to the lack of a comprehensive federal policy. Do
   you think communities need to create more such programs? Why or why not? What would be the advantages
   or disadvantages of communities enacting their own policies to handle immigration problems?

Chapter 4

1. Do you think creating more barriers and redirecting illegal immigration routes into remoter areas of the Southwest are a violation of human rights standards? Use the
   arguments from Maria Jimenez and Mark Krikorian to
   support your answer. Where do you think the blame lies
   for the numerous migrant deaths that result from making
   the cross-border journey more perilous?

2. Many people who reject sterner measures against illegal
   immigrants have voiced the opinion that racism is at the
   heart of these policies. Clayton E. Cramer, however, asserts
   that immigration policy laws should not target the immigrants but the US employers who willingly seek low-pay
   workers. He insists most reformers are driven by a desire
   to fix broken laws, not inflict harm on innocent people
   who have crossed the border to find better lives. Do you
   think Cramer's argument is credible? What evidence can
   you find to support or refute his assertion?

Organizations to Contact

The editors have compiled the following list of organizations concerned with the issues debated in this book. The descriptions are derived from materials provided by the organizations. All have publications or information available for interested readers. The list was compiled on the date of publication of the present volume; the information provided here may change. Be aware that many organizations take several weeks or longer to respond to inquiries, so allow as much time as possible.

American Civil Liberties Union (ACLU)
125 Broad St., 18th Floor, New York, NY   10004
(212) 607-3300 • fax: (212) 607-3318
website: www. aclu.org

The ACLU is an organization dedicated to preserving and upholding the civil rights guaranteed to all people in the United States by the US Constitution and Bill of Rights. With regional offices nationwide, the ACLU seeks to provide all individuals equal services regardless of race, sex, religion, or national origin. The ACLU Immigrants' Rights Project was founded in 1987 specifically to address issues such as detention and deportation, due process, search and seizure, and workplace rights. Information on current projects by the ACLU as well as immigration-related fact sheets, publications, and Supreme Court decisions can be read online.

American Friends Service Committee (AFSC)
1501 Cherry St., Philadelphia, PA   19102
(215) 241-7000 • fax: (215) 241-7275
e-mail: afscinfo@afsc.org
website: www.afsc.org

AFSC is a service organization that seeks to promote development, social justice, and peace worldwide. While the beliefs of the organization are rooted in the Quaker faith, the organization reaches out to individuals of all backgrounds and faiths. AFSC believes that current immigration policies in the United States are inhumane and unfair to individuals who immigrate to the country, even if they lack proper documentation. The AFSC provides publications of its calls for policy reform as well as in-depth reports that explore the issues of legal and illegal immigration.

American Immigration Control Foundation (AICF)

222 W. Main St., Monterey, VA   24465
(540) 468-2022 • fax: (540) 468-2024
e-mail: aicfndn@htcnet.org
website: www.aicfoundation.com

Founded in 1983, the AICF opposes uncontrolled immigration into the United States, believing that it poses a grave threat to the rule of law in the country. The foundation identifies illegal immigration as the greatest threat; however, the organization also advocates for increased governmental control to limit legal immigration. Books, pamphlets, and videos produced by the AICF can be accessed or purchased online.

Center for Immigration Studies (CIS)

1522 K St. NW, Suite 820, Washington, DC   20005-1202
(202) 466-8185 • fax: (202) 466-8076
e-mail: center@cis.org
website: www.cis.org

An independent think tank founded in 1985, CIS examines the ways that immigration affects the United States from economic, social, and demographic viewpoints. The center advocates for immigration policy that takes the national interest into account first, above all other factors. Additionally, CIS supports increased regulation to limit the number of immigrants admitted into the country so that those who are granted citizenship have a greater opportunity to succeed. CIS reports, testimony, and articles cover a variety of topics ranging from immigration history, the costs of immigration, the impact on African Americans, and assimilation of guest workers. All of these publications can be accessed on CIS's website.

Council on Foreign Relations (CFR)

58 E. Sixty-eighth St., New York, NY   10065
(212) 434-9400 • fax: (212) 434-9800
website: www.cfr.org

CFR provides educational information on important foreign policy issues facing the United States. The council does not limit its audience to one specific group, seeking instead to inform everyone from government officials to scholars, journalists to educators, and civic and religious leaders to the average American citizen. CFR does not take official positions on any of the issues that it covers; however, reports and backgrounders published by the council cover many aspects of the immigration debate, and individual scholars do present their own viewpoints in their reports, which cover economic as well as societal and cultural issues. These publications are all available online; *Foreign Affairs* is the official journal of CFR.

Federation for American Immigration Reform (FAIR)

25 Massachusetts Ave. NW, Suite 330, Washington, DC   20001
(202) 328-7004 • fax: (202) 387-3447
website: www.fairus.org

FAIR is a membership organization open to all American citizens who are concerned with the current direction of immigration policy. The organization promotes immigration policy reform that ensures that Americans in the present and the future have the opportunity to achieve happiness and success. FAIR worries that uncontrolled immigration has a negative impact on national security, jobs, health care, education, the environment, and the rule of law, and it encourages lawmakers to consider these impacts carefully when deciding policy. FAIR's website offers reports and fact sheets on numerous immigration-related topics.

The Heritage Foundation

214 Massachusetts Ave. NE, Washington, DC   20002
(202) 546-4400

e-mail: info@heritage.org
website: www.heritage.org

A conservative public policy institute, the Heritage Foundation seeks to promote the ideals of free enterprise, limited government, traditional American values, and a strong national defense. It advocates for an immigration policy that welcomes immigrants who enter the United States through the proper legal channels and imposes restrictions to deter and punish those who enter illegally. Further, the organization believes that the US border must be secure, but border policy must not be so stringent as to restrict commerce. Publications by foundation scholars addressing the issues of immigration can be read online.

John Birch Society
PO Box 8040, Appleton, WI   54912
(920) 749-3780
website: www.jbs.org

Founded in 1958, the John Birch Society is a conservative public policy organization that promotes the principles of personal freedom and limited government. The society works to ensure that no policies passed by the government infringe of the freedoms guaranteed American citizens by the Constitution. Illegal immigration is a great concern to the society, and it advocates for increased governmental restriction and enforcement to curb and control this problem. Reports on suggested legislation to address illegal immigration can be read on the organization's website.

National Council of La Raza (NCLR)
Raul Yzaguirre Bldg., Washington, DC   20036
(202) 785-1670
website: www.nclr.org

NCLR has been working since 1968 to ensure that Hispanic Americans are afforded the same rights and opportunities as all other US citizens. The council is actively involved in policy analysis and advocacy on many immigration-related issues such as the REAL ID Act, comprehensive immigration reform, and the DREAM Act. Reports on these policies and others can be read on the NCLR website along with general immigration facts and policy briefs.

National Immigration Forum

50 F St. NW, Suite 300, Washington, DC   20001
(202) 347-0040 • fax: (202) 347-0058
website: www.immigrationforum.org

The National Immigration Forum was founded in 1982 as an immigrants' rights organization with the goal of ensuring that all those who immigrate to the United States are granted their due rights. The forum seeks to achieve its mission, "To embrace and uphold America's tradition as a nation of immigrants," by reaching out to both policy makers and the American public and encouraging them to engage with the issues of immigration and to support those who seek to establish their families and lives in the United States. Backgrounders, fact sheets, and issue papers can all be downloaded from the forum's website.

National Immigration Law Center (NILC)

3435 Wilshire Blvd., Suite 2850, Los Angeles, CA   90010
(213) 639-3900 • fax: (213) 639-3911
e-mail: info@nilc.org
website: www.nilc.org

NILC works to ensure that the rights of low-income immigrants and their families are protected. Specifically, the center focuses on employment laws and restriction of public services as imposed by the 1996 immigration reform laws. NILC works in many capacities to provide policy analysis, litigation, training and conferences, and publications such as the newsletter *Immigrants' Rights Update*, published eight times a year. Information about the organization's current projects and work can be found on the NILC website.

National Network for Immigrant and Refugee Rights (NNIRR)
310 Eighth St., Suite 303, Oakland, CA   94607
(510) 465-1984 • fax: (510) 465-1885
e-mail: nnirr@nnirr.org
website: www.nnirr.org

NNIRR advocates for a national immigration and refugee policy that is just and that ensures that the rights of all those coming to the United States are observed. To achieve these goals, the network coordinates efforts between local, national, and global groups seeking to improve the conditions of immigrants in the United States. Additionally, NNIRR seeks to educate all individuals about the hardships immigrants face as a result of current US immigration policy. Reports and commentary on immigrant issues in the United States are available on the NNIRR website.

Negative Population Growth (NPG)
2861 Duke St., Suite 36, Alexandria, VA   22314
(703) 370-9510
e-mail: npg@npg.org
website: www.npg.org

NPG believes that in the United States and globally the current levels of population growth are unsustainable and will have a detrimental effect on the world that is already beginning to be apparent. Among the solutions offered to halt population growth in the United States, NPG advocates for policy that allows individuals to enter the country at the same rate that people leave it; so, for example, if two hundred thousand people leave the country each year, then two hundred thousand people will be allowed to immigrate to the country. Reports on these and other issues are accessible on the NPG website.

US Citizenship and Immigration Services (USCIS)
Department of Homeland Security, Washington, DC   20528
(202) 282-8000

website: www.uscis.gov

USCIS is the branch of the US Department of Homeland Security in charge of immigration to the United States. Immigration services, policies, and priorities all originate from the USCIS. Additionally, this government agency also makes decisions regarding who will be allowed to lawfully enter the United States and with what designation; for example, as an immigrant or as a refugee. The USCIS website provides additional information about the services it provides as well as current immigration laws and regulations.

Bibliography of Books

Peter Andreas   *Border Games: Policing the*
                     U.S.-Mexico Divide. Ithaca, NY:
                     Cornell University Press, 2009.

Darrell Ankarlo   *Illegals: The Unacceptable Cost of*
                     America's Failure to Control Its
                     Borders. Nashville: Thomas Nelson,
                     2008.

David Bacon   *Illegal People: How Globalization*
                     Creates Migration and Criminalizes
                     Immigrants. Boston: Beacon, 2008.

Patrick J. Bascio   *On the Immorality of Illegal*
                     Immigration: A Priest Poses an
                     Alternative Christian View.
                     Bloomington, IN: AuthorHouse,
                     2009.

Larry Blasko   *Opening the Borders: Solving the*
                     Mexico/U.S. Immigration Problem for
                     Our Sake and Mexico's. Jamul, CA:
                     Level 4, 2007.

Bill Broyles and   *Desert Duty: On the Line with the*
Mark Haynes   *U.S. Border Patrol.* Austin: University
                     of Texas Press, 2010.

Justin Akers   *No One Is Illegal: Fighting Racism*
Chacón and Mike   *and State Violence on the U.S.-Mexico*
Davis   *Border.* Chicago: Haymarket, 2006.

Aviva Chomsky   *"They Take Our Jobs!": and 20 Other*
                     Myths About Immigration. Boston:
                     Beacon, 2007.

David Coates and Peter Siavelis, eds.   *Getting Immigration Right: What Every American Needs to Know.* Washington, DC: Potomac, 2009.

Roger Daniels   *Guarding the Golden Door: American Immigration Policy and Immigrants Since 1882.* New York: Hill & Wang, 2004.

Kathryn Ferguson, Norma A. Price, and Ted Parks   *Crossing with the Virgin: Stories from the Migrant Trail.* Tucson: University of Arizona Press, 2010.

Otis L. Graham Jr.   *Immigration Reform and America's Unchosen Future.* Bloomington, IN: AuthorHouse, 2008.

J.D. Hayworth with Joe Eule   *Whatever It Takes: Illegal Immigration, Border Security, and the War on Terror.* Washington, DC: Regnery, 2005.

Mark Krikorian   *The New Case Against Immigration: Both Legal and Illegal.* New York: Sentinel, 2008.

Lina Newton   *Illegal, Alien, or Immigrant: The Politics of Immigration Reform.* New York: New York University Press, 2008.

Heather Mac Donald, Victor Davis Hanson, and Steven Malanga   *The Immigration Solution: A Better Plan than Today's.* Chicago: Ivan R. Dee, 2007.

Godfrey Y.
Muwonge

*Immigration Reform: We Can Do It, If
We Apply Our Founders' True Ideals.*
Lanham, MD: University Press of
America, 2010.

Mae M. Ngai

*Impossible Subjects: Illegal Aliens and
the Making of Modern America.*
Princeton, NJ: Princeton University
Press, 2004.

Pia Orrenius
and Madeline
Zavodny

*Beside the Golden Door: U.S.
Immigration Reform in a New Era of
Globalization.* Washington, DC:
American Enterprise Institute, 2010.

William Perez

*We Are Americans: Undocumented
Students Pursuing the American
Dream.* Sterling, VA: Stylus, 2009.

Alejandro Portes
and Rubén G.
Rumbaut

Immigrant America: A Portrait.
Berkeley and Los Angeles: University
of California Press, 2006.

Margaret Regan

*The Death of Josseline: Immigration
Stories from the Arizona Borderlands.*
Boston: Beacon, 2010.

Jason L. Riley

*Let Them In: The Case for Open
Borders.* New York: Gotham, 2008.

David Spener

*Clandestine Crossings: Migrants and
Coyotes on the Texas-Mexico Border.*
Ithaca, NY: Cornell University Press,
2009.

Terry Greene
Sterling

*Illegal: Life and Death in Arizona's
Immigration War Zone.* Guilford, CT:
Lyons, 2010.

Tom Tancredo   *In Mortal Danger: The Battle for America's Border and Security.* Nashville: WND, 2006.

Index

A

ACLU (American Civil Liberties
Union), 123, 124
Aerial drones, 66
African Americans
Loop21.com website, 195
peach-industry workers, 26
Agricultural industry
child labor crackdown, 78
Commission on Agricultural
Workers, 26
false claims, 25
illegal workers, 21, 35, 92–93
Iowa State University study,
26–27
"Special Agricultural Workers"
program, 131
Agriculture and Resource Eco-
nomics Department (UCD), 27
Agriprocessors, Inc., 104
Albania, deportation to, 108
Albayrak, Nebahat, 137
Ali, Ayaan Hirsi, 137, 139–141
ALIPAC (Americans for Legal Im-
migration Political Action
Committee), 195, 196
American Civil Liberties Union
(ACLU), 123, 124, 183
American Immigration Lawyers
Association (AILA), 100, 125
American University School of
International Service, 14
Americans for Legal Immigration
Political Action Committee
(ALIPAC), 195, 196
Amnesty, 138

blanket amnesty (US), 15
burdens of, 16
granting by Clinton/Reagan,
128
Heritage Foundation research,
118
Netherlands discussions, 137–
142
Amuedo-Dorante, Catalina, 133
Anti-immigration protestors
Arizona legislation, 75–76
blame of employers, 204–205
criticism of laws vs. people,
202–205
El Paso, Texas, ss policies, 62
misinformation given by, 50–
51, 59
protesting without permits,
198–199
racism and, 195–200, 201–205
Appleton-Whittell Research Ranch
(Audubon Society), 76
Arizona
anti-immigration legislation,
75–76
Brewer's governorship of, 65–
66, 121, 123–124
drug smuggling, 76
Maricopa County sheriff, 86–
87, 90, 116
onset of illegal immigration,
93
Pima County, 123
sanctuary policy conse-
quences, 116–118, 121
Tucson Sector Border Patrol,
192
US Constitution and, 121–122

232

U

United States (US)
Arizona boycott suggestion,
124–125
asylum for Central American
refugees, 164–165
deportation of illegal immigrants, unrealistic, 101–113
Ellis Island, 20
federal government deficit, 32
sanctuary policy, negatives,
172–177
sanctuary policy, positives,
162–171
See also Great Recession
University of California, Davis
(UCD), 27
University of California, Irvine
(UCI), 49, 60
University of California, Los Angeles (UCLA), 34, 130
University of Illinois, 36
US Chamber of Commerce, 24
USCIS (Citizenship and Immigration Services), 111
US Customs and Border Protection, 108, 110–111, 186, 192
US Department of Justice, 99.106
US Department of Labor, 132–
133, 153
US Immigration and Naturalization Service, 35
US-Mexico border
aerial drone flights, 66
changing nature of, 79
harm to wildlife, 76
illegal immigrant crossing
data, 74
mass deportation, 102

new Mexican immigrants,
70–72
1980s immigration stream,
154
permanent fence solution, 72
"virtual fence," 70
US-VISIT program, 111

V

Van Gogh, Theo, 139, 140
Ventura County Combined
Agency Team, 41
Ventura County (CA) crime,
40–41
Verdonk, Rita, 139
Veteran benefits programs, 32, 35
Villa, Pancho, 95
Virginia, illegal immigration, 83
"Virtual fence" (US-Mexico
border), 70
Voice of The People USA, 198–
199

W

Wales, David, 44
Walker, Devona, 195–199
Wallis, Jim, 123
Wall Street Journal (newspaper),
148
Washington Independent
(newspaper), 16
Washington Post (newspaper), 62,
190
Washington Times (newspaper),
128
Welfare programs, 16, 21, 25, 27,
29, 33
Westat, Inc. survey, 132–133